KU-617-228

THOMAS MIDDLETON

WOMEN BEWARE
WOMEN

Edited by
CHARLES BARBER

OLIVER & BOYD
EDINBURGH
1969

622·3 MID

Yo/YQA

9427

MID 126694

OLIVER AND BOYD LTD

Tweeddale Court

Edinburgh 1

First Published 1969

© 1969—Critical Introduction, Note on the Text, Text as printed, Textual Notes, Commentary, Bibliography, and Glossary—Charles Barber.

Hardback 05 001815 9
Paperback 05 001816 7

Printed in Great Britain by
Hazell Watson & Viney Ltd
Aylesbury, Bucks

THE FOUNTAINWELL DRAMA TEXTS

General Editors

T. A. DUNN

ANDREW GURR

JOHN HORDEN

A. NORMAN JEFFARES

R. L. C. LORIMER

Assistant General Editor

BRIAN W. M. SCOBIE

11

ACKNOWLEDGMENTS

I should like to express my warm gratitude to Dr Andrew Gurr, who acted as Textual General Editor for this volume of the Fountainwell Drama Texts series, and to whom I have constantly turned for advice and help.

I should also like to thank, for their unfailing courtesy and helpfulness, the Librarians and library-staffs of the British Museum, the Victoria and Albert Museum, the Bodleian Library, Trinity College, Cambridge, Worcester College, Oxford, and the University of Leeds.

CHARLES BARBER

Leeds
April 1968

CONTENTS

CRITICAL INTRODUCTION

There is no known reference to *Women Beware Women* before the Stationers' Register entry of 1653, and its date of composition is still disputed. At one time it was held that the play must date from before 1622, because no record has been preserved of its licensing by Sir Henry Herbert, whose office-book begins in 1622; but this argument has been shown to be fallacious.[1] It has also been argued that it must date from 1621 or later, because of a reference to a married couple going to "stock a new found Land"[2]; but this argument too has been shown to be inconclusive.[3] Most critics tend to date the play to the end of Middleton's career (1623–7), on the grounds of its great power and maturity. However, this argument is beginning to lose its force: the evidence for Middleton's authorship of *The Revenger's Tragedy* (c. 1606) is now becoming extremely strong[4], so that we have to take seriously the suggestion that Middleton could write powerful tragedy in the earlier part of his career. An argument has recently been advanced for dating *Women Beware Women* to 1613–14, on the grounds that its image-patterns closely resemble those of *The Triumph of Truth* (mayoral pageant of 1613);[5] but evidence of this kind is not by itself conclusive, and the whole question must still be considered wide open.

The Brancha plot derives ultimately from the true-life story of Bianca Capello, who was born in 1548 of a noble Venetian family, and

[1] G. E. Bentley, *The Jacobean and Caroline Stage*, vol. IV, p. 906. Oxford (Clarendon Press) 1956.

[2] *Women Beware Women* (hereafter cited as *W.B.W.*), I. II. 69. See B. Maxwell, "The Date of Middleton's *Women Beware Women*", in *P.Q.*, XXII (1943), pp. 338–42.

[3] Elizabeth Jacobs, *A Critical Edition of Thomas Middleton's* WOMEN BEWARE WOMEN, pp. lxxiii–lxxiv. Unpublished thesis (University of Wisconsin) 1941.

[4] See especially G. R. Price, "The Authorship and Bibliography of *The Revenger's Tragedy*", in *The Library* (5th series), XV (1960), pp. 262–77; and P. B. Murray, "The Authorship of *The Revenger's Tragedy*", in *Papers of the Bibliographical Society of America*, 56 (1962), pp. 195–218.

[5] J. I. Cope, "The Date of Middleton's *Women Beware Women*", in *M.L.N.*, LXXVI (1961), pp. 295–300.

in 1563 eloped with Pietro Buonaventuri, a Florentine gentleman of the Salviati family, whom she married and by whom she had a daughter. She became the mistress of Francesco de' Medici, at first secretly, and then (after the assassination of her husband in 1569) openly. In 1574 Francesco became Grand Duke of Tuscany. In 1579 his wife died, and he married Bianca, despite the opposition of his brother, the cardinal Ferdinando. Francesco died suddenly of a fever in 1587, and Bianca a few hours after; the cardinal succeeded as Grand Duke.

The story was a well-known one, and Middleton's immediate source for it has not been identified. Dr Karl Christ argued for the eighty-fourth and eighty-fifth stories in the *Ducento Novelle* of Celio Malespini (Venice 1609), finding numerous parallels between them and the play; but he himself admitted that Malespini cannot be the sole source, since he does not deal with the final phases of Bianca's career.[6] Dr J. R. Mulryne suggests that Middleton may have used an un-published portion of Fynes Moryson's *Itinerary* (written c. 1619–20). He also points out that the Bianca story is found in numerous un-published manuscripts; the fourteen that he has examined all give versions of the story closely resembling Malespini's.[7]

Some of Middleton's deviations from historical fact were un-doubtedly suggested by his sources, but these deviations are neverthe-less used by him in characteristic ways. For example, Malespini's Pietro is a merchant's clerk, like Leantio; but Middleton seizes on this point and lays great emphasis on Leantio's poverty and inferior social rank (whereas the historical Pietro Buonaventuri was at any rate a gentleman); in this way he underlines the imprudence of the match, and the social and economic pressures on Brancha. Middleton also compresses events a great deal (in real life they occupied twenty-four years); this may reduce the psychological verisimilitude, by making changes of attitude in the characters take place rather suddenly, but it heightens the dramatic contrasts, and gives a sense of events working themselves out with remorseless logic.

The Isabella-Hippolito plot is probably taken from the *Histoire Veritable des Infortunees et Tragiques Amours d'Hypolite & d'Isabella,*

[6] Karl Christ, *Quellenstudien zu den Dramen Thomas Middletons*, pp. 46–68. Borna-Leipzig 1905. As minor sources of the play, he also points to More's *Utopia* and Kyd's *Spanish Tragedy*.

[7] J. R. Mulryne, *A Critical Edition of Thomas Middleton's "Women Beware Women"*: unpublished thesis, 2 vols, Cambridge 1962. vol. 1, lxxiv–lxxxiv.

Neapolitains (Rouen 1597). An English version was published in 1628, but this was after Middleton's death.

"Like our own Sex, we have no Enemy", says the dying Brancha, and the title of the play expresses the same view. But what the play itself reveals is something quite different: it shows that woman's worst enemy is man, and depicts the perversions to which women become subject when they are simply the property of men in a male-dominated society, a society moreover in which everything has its cash price. Livia, who entraps the other two women, does so on behalf of men—Isabella for Hippolito, and Brancha for the Duke. When she tries to behave like the men, and buy a lover for herself, they very soon put a stop to that, for she lives in a society where there is one rule for men and another for women.

Livia, Brancha, and Isabella all have things to say about the situation of women[8], but it is Isabella who exemplifies most clearly their plight in this society, where they are merely property. She is quite simply sold to the Ward, and her father constantly refers to her expensive education and her courtly accomplishments as a kind of investment, which will get her a rich husband; when Isabella displays her accomplishments before the Duke, Fabritio says to her prospective husband

> Nay, you shall see yong heir, what y'have for your money,
> Without fraud or imposture.[9]

This is the point of the scene where Isabella is "tendered" to the Ward (III. III), in which he and Sordido inspect her as if she were a prize heifer. Most suitors, plainly, would be more tactful than the Ward: but it is his very crudity that allows the audience to see the essence of the situation, undisguised by tact or good manners. Isabella, in her bitter speeches in I. II, expresses most feelingly the situation of women in general in her society—

> Men buy their slaves, but women buy their masters.[10]

The effect on her is shown to be corrupting. She recognises that marriage can be "the most blest estate"[11], and she expresses her resolve to "keep her days true to her husband"[12]; but she ends by

[8] See *W.B.W.*, I. II. 35–40, 44–50, 183–206; II. II. 306–7; III. I. 49–58; III. III 32–6.
[9] *W.B.W.*, III. II. 199–200.   [10] *W.B.W.*, I. II. 200.
[11] *W.B.W.*, I. II. 202.   [12] *W.B.W.*, I. II. 185.

entering eagerly into the disgusting marriage as a cover for a liaison with Hippolito. The trick that Livia plays on her does not put pressure on her to do this: it merely has the effect of revealing to her where her sexual desires really lie, by removing the incest-inhibition. The society around her takes it for granted that a woman married to a rich fool will lay in "more provision for her youth"[13]; and, once Isabella realises what her desires are, she follows the way of the world.

The arranged marriage is disastrous; but so is the love-match of Leantio and Brancha. This is a highly imprudent marriage, given the kind of society they live in, as Leantio's mother makes quite clear in the first scene. At the opening of the play, Brancha is depicted as a rather sensual girl, and she happily brushes aside the social differences between herself and Leantio, and the meanness of her new home, as long as her only idea of bliss is having Leantio in her bed. But once she has discovered sexual satisfaction elsewhere, the poverty of her new way of life becomes intolerable, and she starts demanding silver ewers and gilt casting-bottles: she is corrupted by the desire for wealth and position. It is sometimes said that she becomes a completely different character after her seduction by the Duke[14], but it seems to me rather that we go on learning more about her. At the beginning she is a somewhat enigmatic figure (this is the point of her silent presence on the stage for the first 130 lines of the play), and as the play goes on we keep making discoveries about this seemingly demure young girl. We see her predisposition to be attracted by a middle-aged man when she enquires about the age of the Duke, and remarks that a man is at his best at fifty-five[15]. This bias comes out in the seduction-scene, for, although she pleads with the Duke, she resists him only half-heartedly, and is plainly fascinated by him. After this crisis in her life, we see emerge the traits in her character that had been submerged in her honeymoon sensuality: wilfulness, pertness, irresponsibility, quickness of wit, and a certain hardness. We hear that she could wrangle for what she wanted when she was two hours old[16]. An unexpected coarseness appears when she comments on Fabritio's use of the word *breast*[17]. We see her as the great court lady, bandying

---

[13] *W.B.W.*, III. II. 137.
[14] See *e.g.* W. Empson, *Some Versions of Pastoral*, p. 55. London (Chatto & Windus) 1935.
[15] *W.B.W.*, I. III. 103–4.   [16] *W.B.W.*, III. I. 59–60.
[17] *W.B.W.*, III. II. 178–81.

bawdry about watches, and winning a competition in cattiness with Leantio (the kept man and the kept woman). But her success goes to her head: she becomes a dabbler in high political intrigue and poison (illustrating the contemporary belief that adultery led to murder), and overreaches herself.

Livia is the worldly-wise widow who has no illusions about the position of women in her society; she has buried two husbands and has no intention of putting herself in the power of a third. Nevertheless, her intellect, her subtlety, and her mastery of intrigue are put at the disposal of men, with no reward to herself. When she falls in love with Leantio, she quite blatantly buys him as her lover, just as the Ward had bought Isabella as his wife and the Duke had bought Brancha as his mistress. But she lives in a world where men make the rules: they feel little compunction about seducing women, but cannot tolerate the seduction of their own female relatives, as this is a stain on their honour; and so Hippolito challenges Leantio, and (as the Duke knows) the petty-bourgeois Leantio stands no chance against Hippolito, the gentleman trained in arms. While he is waiting to accost Leantio, Hippolito betrays a faint uneasiness about the inconsistency of his position, which he glosses over in a way that shows that his ideal of honour is concerned only with appearances[18]; but he manifests a complete blindness, amounting to stupidity, to the vulnerability of his situation, because he blandly assumes that Livia will accept the male point of view: he thinks that he will only have to invoke the family honour to get her to acquiesce in the murder of her lover, and when instead she turns viciously on him and exposes his affair with Isabella he is genuinely surprised and hurt:

> Here's a care
> Of reputation, and a Sisters fortune
> Sweetly rewarded by her.[19]

The inconsistency of the masculine position is also illustrated by Guardiano and Leantio. Guardiano has no compunction about arranging rape or seduction, but the moment he hears that his own nephew's wife has committed adultery, he is ready to plot murder. Leantio taunts Brancha with the word "whore", but the woman that he himself sleeps with is "a beauteous Benefactor"[20].

[18] *W.B.W.*, IV. II. 4–10.   [19] *W.B.W.*, IV. II. 160–2.
[20] *W.B.W.*, IV. I. 87.

The men of the play assume that women are property. In one curious passage[21], Leantio compares himself to a hoarding miser, and the Duke to a spendthrift prodigal, both of them damned; the "wealth" that they have hoarded and squandered is of course Brancha. Leantio constantly talks of Brancha as a treasure, a gem, something that must be kept locked up in a chest, something that he has stolen; unfortunately for him, the Duke can outbid him for the purchase of this property. It is a mercenary society, where everything has its price. Leantio accepts the captainship as payment for his cuckolding. Guardiano has spent the past fifteen years acting as court-pander, as the path to riches and advancement[22]. Even the fiery Hippolito has to have a material incentive to the killing of Leantio; in the Renaissance view, a gentleman's sense of honour ought to be sufficient to impel him to kill his sister's lover, but the Duke does not trust to this alone, and dangles before Hippolito the rich match between Vincentio and Livia, to which Hippolito frequently refers. The Duke himself is a monstrous egotist—

> I affect
> A passionate pleading, 'bove an easie yeilding,
> But never pitied any, they deserve none
> That will not pity me.[23]

It is self-evident to him that any woman who does not yield to him deserves to be punished without pity.

It is not only a mercenary world: it is also a world of isolation and loneliness, a world of strangers. *Strange* and *stranger* are recurrent words in the play: *stranger* occurs eighteen times (compared with an average of less than two occurrences per play in Shakespeare), while *strange*, *strangely*, and *strangest* occur twenty-one times (compared with an average of about seven per play in Shakespeare). It is frequently emphasised that Brancha is a stranger (foreigner) in Florence; and when she is dying, Middleton evokes poignantly her sense of isolation:

> What make I here? these are all strangers to me,
> Not known but by their malice.[24]

The closest social tie, that of kinship, is ineffectual in producing neighbourly conduct. Livia entraps her niece Isabella as well as the stranger Brancha; indeed, to do so she actually makes use of her kin-

---

[21] *W.B.W.*, III. II. 101–6.   [22] *W.B.W.*, II. II. 24–50.
[23] *W.B.W.*, II. II. 426–9.   [24] *W.B.W.*, V. II. 225–6.

ship with Isabella; and she does it by making Isabella believe that Hippolito is a stranger (not a kinsman).[25]

Other recurrent words in the play which link up with *stranger* are *cunning*, *subtle*, and *spiteful*. Against these is pitted a group of words to do with benevolence and hospitality, like *pity*, *friend*, and *neighbour*. There is frequent reference to "house-keeping", the generous hospitality of the great house, and to neighbourliness of conduct, as in Livia's:

> Oh what's become
> Of the true hearty love was wont to be
> 'Mongst Neighbours in old time?[26]

This however is in the past; in the present, friendship is a mere pretence, a hypocritical cover for intrigue and betrayal: all of Livia's hearty neighbourliness to Leantio's mother is just a ploy to entrap Brancha. In the society depicted by the play there is no neighbourliness, but isolated individuals scheming against one another and competing for sex, money, and power.[27]

The characters of the play are notable for their remoteness from theatrical cliché: there are no whores with hearts of gold, bluff honest soldiers, and so on. Instead, there is close and unsentimental observation of the real world, and remarkable psychological penetration; as a small example of this, one could point to the handling of Leantio in the latter part of the play, when his lacerated pride impels him (and not only once) to seek out Brancha, to prove to her that he does not need her love. Middleton's attitude to his characters is one of complete detachment: we understand their plight, and may pity their misfortunes, but we are never invited to identify with them; the method in fact is what it is nowadays fashionable to call "alienation" (after Brecht's *Verfremdung*). There is no danger (as there is in some Jacobean tragedies) that the audience will become morally confused

[25] The use of the word "stranger" in the play has been discussed by R. B. Parker, "Middleton's Experiments with Comedy and Judgment", in *Jacobean Theatre*, (*Stratford-upon-Avon Studies* I), ed. J. R. Brown and B. Harris, pp. 179–99. London (Edward Arnold) 1960.

[26] *W.B.W.*, II. II. 249–51.

[27] There is no room here to discuss the other significant clusters of words and images in the play; for these, see especially M. C. Bradbrook, *Themes and Conventions of Elizabethan Tragedy*, pp. 224–39 and C. Ricks, "Word-Play in *Women Beware Women*", in *R.E.S.*, (N.S.) XII (1961), pp. 238–50.

because their sympathies have been caught up by morally ambiguous characters, for the personages are seen in an ironic light, and dramatic irony is a major method of the play. The detachment and the irony give the play affinities with comedy; and indeed there are passages which are splendidly comic, like the scene where Leantio returns to Brancha and receives an unexpected kind of welcome—

> Alas Sir,
> Think of the world, how we shall live, grow serious,
> We have been married a whole fortnight now.[28]

Even at the end of the play, when characters are destroying one another wholesale, there is the minor comedy of the Duke puzzling all the time over the synopsis of the masque, because it fails to tally with the events on-stage.

The ending of the play has often been severely criticised, on the grounds that it is purely conventional melodrama in the revenge-tradition, and is out of keeping with the more naturalistic mode of the earlier acts.[29] It certainly carries to an extreme the compression of events which is typical of the whole play; and some of the deaths do seem rather casual (especially the Duke's). Nevertheless, the audience surely does feel that the fate of the characters is an inevitable consequence of their self-seeking: in a society of unscrupulous individualism, there is no peace or security for anybody. Very striking in the last act is the sanguine belief of the various plotters that they can commit murder and get away with it, simply because it is a time of revels. This is insisted on so often, and is so fatuous (murder by poisoned arrows, for example, being rather obviously non-accidental), that it makes us feel that the characters are blinded and doomed. Because of the detachment and the irony, the final disaster evokes pity rather than terror; but it does this with considerable intensity.

From Nathaniel Richards's prefatory verses, it is clear that the play had been produced on the pre-Commonwealth stage, and had been

---

[28] *W.B.W.*, III. I. 174–6.

[29] See *e.g.* G. R. Hibbard, "The Tragedies of Thomas Middleton and the Decadence of the Drama", in *Nottingham Renaissance and Modern Studies*, vol. I, pp. 35–64. Nottingham (Nottingham U.P.) 1957. For a different view of the ending, see R. B. Parker, "Middleton's Experiments with Comedy and Judgment", *op. cit.* (fn. 25 above).

successful; but we do not know when or where. It was not revived at the Restoration, and Genest has no record of any performance between 1660 and 1830.[30] The play was produced by the Royal Shakespeare Company at the Arts Theatre, London, in 1962, opening on 4 July; the producer was Anthony Page. There has also been a television production of the play, by Granada Television, transmitted on 11 January 1965; the producer was Philip Mackie and the director Gordon Flemyng. The play was produced at the Traverse Theatre Club, Edinburgh, from 20 February to 16 March 1968; the producer was Gordon McDougall.

[30] John Genest, *Some Account of the English Stage from the Restoration in 1660 to 1830*, 10 vols. Bath 1832.

A NOTE ON THE TEXT

On 9 September 1653, a list of forty-one plays was entered in the Stationers' Register by "Master Mosely"[1]; it included the following group:

More Dissemblers besides women
A right woman, or women beware of women
No witt, no helpe like a woman   } Mr Tho. Midleton
The Puritan Maid, modest wife & wanton
   widdow, by

Bentley points out[2] that *A Right Woman* is not an appropriate alternative title for *Women Beware Women*, and that Moseley entered *A Right Woman* again in 1660, as a comedy by Beaumont and Fletcher; the double title in the 1653 entry was probably an attempt by Moseley to get two plays registered for one fee.

In 1657 Moseley published an octavo volume called *Two New Playes*, containing *More Dissemblers Besides Women* and *Women Beware Women*. Jacobs has shown, by an examination of the ornaments used, that the printer was Thomas Newcomb, who was more than once employed by Moseley.[3] The collation is A^4 $B-N^8$ O^4. On A1 is the general title-page, which reads as follows: TWO NEW | PLAYES. | *VIZ.* [Brace extending over four lines of play titles] More DISSEMBLERS | besides WOMEN. | WOMEN beware | WOMEN. | [Rule] | WRITTEN | by *Tho. Middleton*, Gent. | [Rule] | [Ornament] | [Rule] | *London*, Printed for *Humphrey Moseley* and are to be sold | at his shop at the Prince's Arms in St. *Pauls* | Churchyard. 1657. |

A1v is blank, A2 is the title-page for *More Dissemblers Besides Women*, and A2v is blank. On A3 and A3v there is a prose address to the reader, on A4 a poem about *Women Beware Women* by Nathaniel Richards, and on A4v "The Actors Names" (for *More Dissemblers Besides Women*). The text of *More Dissemblers Besides*

---

[1] *A Transcript of the Registers of the Worshipful Company of Stationers: From 1640–1708 A.D.*, [ed. G. E. B. Eyre], 3 vols, vol. 1, pp. 428–9. London (privately printed) 1913–14.

[2] *Op. cit.*, p. 906.   [3] *Op. cit.*, pp. xvi–xviii.

Women begins on B1 and ends on G2. G2v is blank, and on G3 is the title-page of *Women Beware Women*, as follows: WOMEN | BE-WARE | WOMEN. | [Rule] | A | TRAGEDY, | BY | *Tho. Middleton*, Gent. | [Rule] | [Ornament] | [Rule] | LONDON: | Printed for *Humphrey Moseley*, 1657. |

On G3v is a list of characters, and the text itself begins on G4 and continues to O3. O3v, O4, and O4v are blank. The pages of the volume are numbered from 1 to 197, beginning on B1, but with pages 142 (K7v) and 143 (K8r) mistakenly numbered 140 and 141. In the two copies in the Dyce Collection there is a portrait of Middleton facing A1.

I have collated eight copies of *Two New Plays*: two in the British Museum (643.b.37 and 162.d.28), two in the Victoria and Albert Museum (6567.17.P.28 and 29), two in the Bodleian Library (Malone 247 and Art 8⁰ C 19 BS), one at Trinity College, Cambridge, and one at Worcester College, Oxford. In *Women Beware Women*, I have found in these eight copies a total of 55 substantial press-variants, distributed among four formes: G outer (one variant, three copies in the uncorrected state); G inner (one variant, three copies in the uncorrected state); I inner (19 variants on five pages, one copy in the uncorrected state); and M inner (thirty-four variants on eight pages, one copy in the uncorrected state). All but 9 of the 55 corrections are changes in punctuation; some of these are obviously necessary but many of them are not: these latter represent the imposition on the text of a heavier style of punctuation than Middleton himself was in the habit of using, and in such cases I usually retain the uncorrected reading as being more likely to be Middleton's own.[4]

The play was set up from a carefully prepared copy, and offers a good text. It seems unlikely that it was a theatrical prompt copy: the stage directions, admittedly, are pretty full, but some essential ones are missing (especially in the final scene), and many of the entrances are marked late. With one exception, there is nothing in the play that looks like an instruction or advance warning to actors or effects-men;

---

[4] For her unpublished edition, Jacobs collated four copies of *Two New Plays* in the United States. She found six press-variants (in H Inner, H Outer, and I Outer) absent from any of the eight copies I have examined; I have recorded these in my textual notes. Mulryne, for his unpublished edition, collated all 19 extant copies of *Two New Plays*; he lists a further two press-variants in H Inner; these also I have recorded in my Textual Notes.

the exception is *Table and Chess*[5], to which we should just possibly add *Duke above* and *Cupids shoot*[6]. These suggest that the printer's copy may have been prepared from a playhouse manuscript, even though it was not one itself.

The printer's copy was a scribal transcript, not a Middleton holograph. This can be seen by comparing the punctuation and spelling with those in the manuscript of *A Game at Chess* in the library of Trinity College, Cambridge, which is in Middleton's own hand: both the punctuation and the spelling of *Women Beware Women* are markedly different from Middleton's own usage. The following is a sample of the evidence from spelling, using G as shorthand for the Trinity manuscript of *A Game at Chess*, and W for the 1657 edition of *Women Beware Women*.

For final unstressed *-y*, G prefers *-ie* (over 93%), whereas W uses *-y* (96%). In G, final *-l* is invariably doubled after a short vowel; in W, it is usually doubled when the syllable is stressed, but not when it is unstressed (single *-l* in over 98% of the cases). For *be, he, me, she,* and *we*, G nearly always has *bee, hee, mee, shee,* and *wee* (nearly 99% of cases); W on the other hand has only one of these long forms out of a total of 676 examples. G prefers the digraphs *ay* and *oy* to *ai* and *oi*, even in non-final position, where *ay* and *oy* account for over 98% of the examples; the corresponding figures for W are 55% for *oy* and less than 1% for *ay*. For the suffix *-ness*, G regularly uses *-nes* (62 examples), and occasionally *-nesse* (5 examples); W invariably uses *-ness*. For *nk*, G uses the spelling *nck* (except in *thinke* and *thanke*); W invariably uses *nk*. G quite often uses the ligature æ, especially in the prefix *præ-*; no examples of this occur in W (except in the word *Scæn.* in scene-headings, and this is probably intended to be Latin). In a number of words, G favours a spelling with ʒ, e.g. *suffiʒe, exerciʒe, practiʒe, sacrifiʒe,* and *riʒe*; but W invariably uses *s* or *c* in these words, though there are two cases where the rhyme suggests that the original spelling had ʒ[7].

In the past tenses and past participles of regular weak verbs, G uses nine different endings, with a clear pattern of preferences for the positions in which each occurs. The ending *-t* is the usual form after voiceless consonants (except /t/), as in *fixt*; a less common variant is *-te*, which occurs occasionally after /p/, /f/, and /k/, as in *lookte*; an

[5] *W.B.W.*, II. II. 201. [6] *W.B.W.*, II. II. 368, V. II. 143.
[7] See notes to IV. II. 259–60 and V. II. 43–5.

even rarer variant is -'*t*, which occurs only after /ʃʃ/, as in *wash't*. The ending -'*st* is used when the spelling is *c* and the pronunciation /s/, as in *plac'st*. The ending -*ed* is normal after /t/ and /d/, and also occurs occasionally in other positions, especially after a liquid, a nasal, or a vowel. After voiced sounds (except /d/), the normal endings are -*de* and -*d*; of these, -*d* is especially favoured after /b/, /g/, /dʒ/, /l/, /n/, /ŋ/, and /ər/, while -*de* is commoner after vowels, after vowel + /r/ (excluding /ər/), and after /m/, /v/, and /z/; so for example we find *blabd* but *ceaʒde*. The endings -'*d* and -'*de* are rare, occurring only twice each. In W, the pattern is quite different: the ending -*ed* is used in much the same way as in G, but this is to be expected (since it represents a pronunciation /id/); and the really common ending in W is -'*d*, which accounts for 62% of the cases; the endings -*d* and -*de* are very rare, while the endings -*te*, -'*de*, and -'*st* do not occur at all.

Examples of single words which regularly differ in spelling in the two texts include the following: G *agen*, W *again*; G *bergayne*, W *bargain*; G *bewtie*, W *beauty*; G *bloud*, W *blood*; G *closse*, W *close*; G *deere*, W *dear*; G *ynough*, W *enough*; G *e'en*, W *ev'n*; G *frend*, W *friend*; G *hower*, W *hour*; G *Ide, Ime, Ile*, W *I'ld, I'm, I'll*; G *litle*, W *little*; G *mistris*, W *mistress*; G *nere, ne're*, W *nev'r, ne'r*; G *ould*, W *old*; G *plauge*, W *plague*; G *strenght*, W *strength*; G *strickt*, W *strict*; G *weere*, W *w'are*; G *weomen*, W *women*.

There are also points on which the two texts agree in spelling. However, one would expect this even in two texts chosen at random; and, in the absence of a large-scale statistical analysis of general spelling frequencies in the period, it is impossible to be absolutely certain whether the resemblances between G and W are greater than could be expected from chance alone. What certainly can be said, however, is that *Women Beware Women* is not recognisable at all as a Middleton text in its spellings. These spellings, moreover, are decidedly more "modern" than Middleton's own; this modernization might be due solely to the compositors, but it seems more likely that such a thorough-going normalisation is due to a scribal transcription.[8]

[8] The other play in *Two New Playes* has spellings very similar to those of *W.B.W.*, which might suggest that the spellings are due solely to the compositor, not to a scribe. But, if Moseley obtained two very old copies of the plays, they may well have needed to be transcribed before being given to the printer, in which case the same scribe could well have copied both plays. And the spellings are so remote from Middleton's that it is difficult to believe that the compositors had his holograph before them.

My working assumption has been that the printer's copy was a scribal transcription made specially for the purpose in the 1650's, and that the scribe tidied up the text and to a considerable extent imposed his own spellings and punctuation on it. It is difficult to guess exactly what kind of copy the scribe himself worked from, but (as suggested on p. 13 above) there are slight indications that it may have been a copy marked for playhouse use; whether or not it was a Middleton holograph is very much an open question.[9]

As my copy-text for this edition, I have used *Two New Playes*, British Museum 643.b.37. The following silent alterations have been made: (1) The letter "s" has been substituted for "long s" wherever it occurs; (2) At the end of a complete speech, where no suspension is intended, a full-point has been inserted where omitted (or where replaced by comma, semi-colon, or colon); (3) Faulty capitalisation (at the beginning of a line of verse, or at the beginning of a proper name) has been regularised in accordance with normal Jacobean usage; (4) Speech-prefixes are set in caps, and are given in full and always in the same form; (5) The names of characters have been similarly normalised in stage directions and in the list of Dramatis Personae; (6) Additional stage directions, or additions to existing ones, have been provided within pointed brackets; (7) In the Dramatis Personae, typography and punctuation have been regularised.

All other departures from the copy-text are recorded in the textual notes. The emendations of other editors are not usually recorded unless they have been adopted into the present text. The textual notes do however record all the substantial press-variants that I have found in the eight copies of the 1657 edition that I have examined. Those variants which substantially affect the reading of the text are given as footnotes; the remainder are gathered in the section at the back.

[9] A few typically Middletonian forms occur in the text: *e.g.* the spellings *enclines* (with *en-*), *vitious*, *Fabritio* (with *-t-*), *wisemen*, *yongmans*; and the use of 2. and 3. as speech-prefixes (I. III). But these occur very sparsely, and are not sufficient to prove that the scribe copied from a Middleton holograph.

The Tragedy of

My Familiar Acquaintance,

THO. MIDDLETON.

WOmen beware Women; 'tis a true Text
Never to be forgot: Drabs of State vext,
Have Plots, Poysons, Mischeifs that seldom miss,
To murther Vertue with a venom kiss.
Witness this worthy *Tragedy*, exprest
By him that well deserv'd among the best
Of *Poets* in his time: He knew the rage,
Madness of Women crost; and for the Stage
Fitted their humors, Hell-bred Malice, Strife
Acted in State, presented to the life.
I that have seen't, can say, having just cause,
Never came *Tragedy* off with more applause.

Nath. Richards.

⟨DRAMATIS PERSONAE⟩

DUKE *of Florence*

LORD CARDINAL, *Brother to the* DUKE

TWO CARDINALS *more*

A LORD

FABRITIO, *Father to* ISABELLA

HIPPOLITO, *Brother to* FABRITIO

GUARDIANO, *Uncle to the Foolish* WARD

The WARD, *a rich yong Heir*

LEANTIO, *a Factor, Husband to* BRANCHA

SORDIDO, *the* WARDS *Man*

⟨A PAGE⟩

LIVIA, *Sister to* FABRITIO

ISABELLA, *Neece to* LIVIA

BRANCHA, LEANTIO'S *Wife*

WIDOW, *his* MOTHER

⟨TWO LADIES⟩

STATES *of Florence*, ⟨KNIGHTS⟩, CITIZENS, *A* PRENTICE, BOYS, MESSENGER, SERVANTS

⟨*Figures in the Masques:* HYMEN, GANYMED, HEBE, *and* CUPIDS.⟩

The Scæn.
FLORENCE.

ACT I

SCENE I

Enter LEANTIO *with* BRANCHA, *and* MOTHER.

MOTHER. THy sight was never yet more precious to me;
  Welcome with all the affection of a Mother,
  That comfort can express from natural love:
  Since thy birth-joy, a Mothers chiefest gladness,
  After sh'as undergone her curse of sorrows,   5
  Thou was't not more dear to me, then this hour
  Presents thee to my heart. Welcome again.
LEANTIO. 'Las poor affectionate Soul, how her joys speak to me!
  I have observ'd it often, and I know it is
  The fortune commonly of knavish Children   10
  To have the lovingst Mothers.
MOTHER. What's this Gentlewoman?
LEANTIO. Oh you have nam'd the most unvaluedst purchase,
  That youth of man had ever knowledge of.
  As often as I look upon that treasure,   15
  And know it to be mine, (there lies the blessing)
  It joys me that I ever was ordain'd
  To have a Being, and to live 'mongst men;
  Which is a fearful living, and a poor one;
  Let a man truly think on't.   20
  To have the toyl and griefs of fourscore years
  Put up in a white sheet, ti'd with two knots;
  Methinks it should strike Earthquakes in Adulterers,
  When ev'n the very sheets they commit sin in,
  May prove, for ought they know, all their last Garments.   25
  Oh what a mark were there for women then!
  But beauty able to content a Conquerer,
  Whom Earth could scarce content, keeps me in compass;
  I finde no wish in me bent sinfully
  To this mans sister, or to that mans wife: 30
  In loves name let 'em keep their honesties,

And cleave to their own husbands, 'tis their duties.
Now when I go to Church, I can pray handsomely;
Not come like Gallants onely to see faces,
As if Lust went to market still on Sondays.   35
I must confess I am guilty of one sin, Mother,
More then I brought into the world with me;
But that I glory in: 'Tis theft, but noble,
As ever greatness yet shot up withal.
MOTHER.   How's that?   40
LEANTIO.   Never to be repented (Mother,)
　　Though sin be death; I had di'd, if I had not sin'd,
　　And here's my master-peece: Do you now behold her!
　　Look on her well, she's mine, look on her better:
　　Now say, if't be not the best peece of theft   45
　　That ever was committed; and I have my pardon for't:
　　'Tis seal'd from Heaven by marriage.
MOTHER.   Married to her!
LEANTIO.   You must keep councel Mother, I am undone else;
　　If it be known, I have lost her; do but think now   50
　　What that loss is, life's but a triffle to't.
　　From *Venice*, her consent and I have brought her
　　From Parents great in wealth, more now in rage;
　　But let storms spend their furies, now we have got
　　A shelter o'r our quiet innocent loves,   55
　　We are contented; little money sh'as brought me.
　　View but her face, you may see all her dowry,
　　Save that which lies lockt up in hidden vertues,
　　Like Jewels kept in Cabinets.
MOTHER.   Y'are too blame,   60
　　If your obedience will give way to a check,
　　To wrong such a perfection.
LEANTIO.   How?
MOTHER.   Such a Creature,
　　To draw her from her fortune, which no doubt,   65
　　At the full time, might have prov'd rich and noble:
　　You know not what you have done; my life can give you
　　But little helps, and my death lesser hopes.
　　And hitherto your own means has but made shift
　　To keep you single, and that hardly too.   70

What ableness have you to do her right then
In maintenance fitting her birth and vertues?
Which ev'ry woman of necessity looks for,
And most to go above it, not confin'd
By their conditions, vertues, bloods, or births,   75
But flowing to affections, wills, and humors.
LEANTIO.   Speak low sweet Mother; you are able to spoil as many
As come within the hearing: If it be not
Your fortune to mar all, I have much marvel.
I pray do not you teach her to rebel,   80
When she's in a good way to obedience,
To rise with other women in commotion
Against their husbands, for six Gowns a year,
And so maintain their cause, when they'r once up,
In all things else that require cost enough.   85
They are all of 'em a kinde of spirits soon rais'd,
But not so soon laid (Mother). As for example,
A womans belly is got up in a trice,
A simple charge ere it be laid down again:
So ever in all their quarrels, and their courses.   90
And I'm a proud man, I hear nothing of 'em,
They'r very still, I thank my happiness,
And sound asleep; pray let not your tongue wake 'em.
If you can but rest quiet, she's contented
With all conditions, that my fortunes bring her to;   95
To keep close as a wife that loves her husband;
To go after the rate of my ability,
Not the licentious swindg of her own will.
Like some of her old school-fellows, she intends
To take out other works in a new Sampler,   100
And frame the fashion of an honest love,
Which knows no wants; but mocking poverty
Brings forth more children, to make rich men wonder
At divine Providence, that feeds mouths of Infants,
And sends them none to feed, but stuffs their rooms   105
With fruitful bags, their beds with barren wombs.
Good Mother, make not you things worse then they are,
Out of your too much openness; pray take heed on't;
Nor imitate the envy of old people,

That strive to mar good sport, because they are perfit.   110
I would have you more pitiful to youth,
Especially to your own flesh and blood.
I'll prove an excellent husband, here's my hand,
Lay in provision, follow my business roundly,
And make you a Grand-mother in forty weeks.   115
Go, pray salute her, bid her welcome cheerfully.
MOTHER.   Gentlewoman, thus much is a debt of courtesie

⟨*Kisses her.*⟩

Which fashionable strangers pay each other
At a kinde meeting; then there's more then one
Due to the knowledge I have of your neerness.   120

⟨*Kisses her again.*⟩

I am bold to come again, and now salute you
By th'name of daughter, which may challenge more
Then ordinary respect.

⟨*Kisses her a third time.*⟩

LEANTIO.   Why this is well now,
And I think few Mothers of threescore will mend it.   125
MOTHER.   What I can bid you welcome to, is mean;
But make it all your own; we are full of wants,
And cannot welcome worth.
LEANTIO.   Now this is scurvy,
And spake as if a woman lack'd her teeth.   130
These old folks talk of nothing but defects,
Because they grow so full of 'em themselves.
BRANCHA.   Kinde Mother, there is nothing can be wanting
To her that does enjoy all her desires.
Heaven send a quiet peace with this mans love,   135
And I am as rich, as Vertue can be poor;
Which were enough after the rate of minde,
To erect Temples for content plac'd here;
I have forsook Friends, Fortunes, and my Country,
And hourly I rejoyce in't. Here's my Friends,   140
And few is the good number; thy successes
How ere they look, I will still name my fortunes,

Hopeful or spightful, they shall all be welcome:
Who invites many guests, has of all sorts,
As he that trafficks much, drinks of all fortunes,   145
Yet they must all be welcome, and us'd well.
I'll call this place the place of my birth now,
And rightly too; for here my love was born,
And that's the birth day of a womans joys.
⟨*To* LEANTIO.⟩   You have not bid me welcome since I came.   150
LEANTIO.   That I did questionless.
BRANCHA.   No sure, how was't?
  I have quite forgot it.
LEANTIO.   Thus.   ⟨*Kisses her.*⟩
BRANCHA.   Oh Sir, 'tis true;   155
  Now I remember well: I have done thee wrong,
  Pray tak't again Sir.   ⟨*Kisses him.*⟩
LEANTIO.   How many of these wrongs
  Could I put up in an hour? and turn up the Glass
  For twice as many more.   160
MOTHER.   Wilt please you to walk in daughter?
BRANCHA.   Thanks sweet Mother;
  The voice of her that bare me, is not more pleasing.

          Exeunt ⟨BRANCHA *and* MOTHER.⟩

LEANTIO.   Though my own care, and my rich Masters trust,
  Lay their commands both on my Factorship,   165
  This day and night, I'll know no other business
  But her and her dear welcome. 'Tis a bitterness
  To think upon to morrow, that I must leave her
  Still to the sweet hopes of the weeks end,
  That pleasure should be so restrain'd and curb'd   170
  After the course of a rich Work-master,
  That never pays till Saturday night.
  Marry it comes together in a round sum then,
  And do's more good you'll say: Oh fair ey'd *Florence*!
  Didst thou but know, what a most matchless Jewel   175
  Thou now art Mistress of, a pride would take thee,
  Able to shoot destruction through the bloods
  Of all thy youthful Sons; but 'tis great policy
  To keep choice treasures in obscurest places:

Should we shew Theeves our wealth, 'twould make 'em bolder; 180
Temptation is a Devil will not stick
To fasten upon a Saint; take heed of that;
The Jewel is cas'd up from all mens eyes.
Who could imagine now a Gem were kept,
Of that great value under this plain roof? 185
But how in times of absence? what assurance
Of this restraint then; yes, yes? there's one with her.
Old Mothers know the world; and such as these,
When Sons lock Chests, are good to look to Keys.

                                                  Exit.

SCENE II

Enter GUARDIANO, FABRITIO, *and* LIVIA.

GUARDIANO.   What has your daughter seen him yet? know you
  that?
FABRITIO.   No matter, she shall love him.
GUARDIANO.   Nay let's have fair play,
  He has been now my Ward some fifteen year,
  And 'tis my purpose (as time calls upon me)   5
  By custom seconded, and such moral vertues,
  To tender him a wife; now Sir, this wife
  I'ld fain elect out of a daughter of yours.
  You see my meaning's fair; if now this daughter
  So tendered (let me come to your own phrase Sir)   10
  Should offer to refuse him, I were hansell'd.
  ⟨*Aside.*⟩ Thus am I fain to calculate all my words,
  For the Meridian of a foolish old man,
  To take his understanding: What do you answer Sir?
FABRITIO.   I say still she shall love him.   15
GUARDIANO.   Yet again?
  And shall she have no reason for this love?
FABRITIO.   Why do you think that women love with reason?
GUARDIANO. ⟨*Aside.*⟩   I perceive Fools are not at all hours
  foolish,
  No more then wisemen wise.   20

FABRITIO.   I had a wife,
  She ran mad for me; she had no reason for't,
  For ought I could perceive: What think you Lady Sister?
GUARDIANO. ⟨*Aside.*⟩   'Twas a fit match that,
  Being both out of their wits: A loving wife, it seem'd   25
  She strove to come as near you as she could.
FABRITIO.   And if her daughter prove not mad for love too,
  She takes not after her; nor after me,
  If she prefer reason before my pleasure,
  Your an experienc'd widow, Lady Sister,   30
  I pray let your opinion come amongst us.
LIVIA.   I must offend you then, if truth will do't,
  And take my Neeces part, and call't injustice
  To force her love to one she never saw.
  Maids should both see, and like; all little enough;   35
  If they love truly after that, 'tis well.
  Counting the time, she takes one man till death,
  That's a hard task, I tell you; but one may
  Enquire at three years end, amongst yong wives,
  And mark how the game goes.   40
FABRITIO.   Why, is not man
  Tide to the same observance, Lady Sister,
  And in one woman?
LIVIA.   'Tis enough for him;
  Besides he tastes of many sundry dishes   45
  That we poor wretches never lay our lips to;
  As Obedience forsooth, Subjection, Duty, and such Kickshaws,
  All of our making, but serv'd in to them;
  And if we lick a finger, then sometimes
  We are not too blame: Your best Cooks use it.   50
FABRITIO.   Th'art a sweet Lady, Sister, and a witty—
LIVIA.   A witty! Oh the bud of commendation
  Fit for a Girl of sixteen; I am blown man,
  I should be wise by this time; and for instance,
  I have buried my two husbands in good fashion,   55
  And never mean more to marry.
GUARDIANO.   No, why so Lady?
LIVIA.   Because the third shall never bury me:
  I think I am more then witty; how think you Sir?

FABRITIO.   I have paid often fees to a Counsellor   60
  Has had a weaker brain.
LIVIA.   Then I must tell you,
  Your money was soon parted.
GUARDIANO.   Light her now Brother.
LIVIA.   Where is my Neece? let her be sent for straight.   65
  If you have any hope, 'twill prove a wedding;
  'Tis fit y'faith she should have one sight of him,
  And stop upon't, and not be joyn'd in haste,
  As if they went to stock a new found Land.
FABRITIO.   Look out her Uncle, and y'are sure of her,   70
  Those two are nev'r asunder, they've been heard
  In Argument at midnight, Moon-shine nights
  Are Noon days with them; they walk out their sleeps;
  Or rather at those hours, appear like those
  That walk in 'em, for so they did to me.   75
  Look you, I told you truth; they're like a chain,
  Draw but one link, all follows.

Enter HIPPOLITO, *and* ISABELLA *the Neece.*

GUARDIANO.   Oh affinity,
  What peece of excellent workmanship art thou?
  'Tis work clean wrought; for there's no lust, but love in't,   80
  And that abundantly: when in stranger things,
  There is no love at all, but what lust brings.
FABRITIO.   On with your Mask, for 'tis your part to see now,
  And not be seen: Go too, make use of your time;
  See what you mean to like; nay, and I charge you,   85
  Like what you see: Do you hear me? there's no dallying;
  The Gentleman's almost twenty, and 'tis time
  He were getting lawful heirs, and you a breeding on 'em.
ISABELLA.   Good Father!
FABRITIO.   Tell not me of tongues and rumors.   90
  You'll say the Gentleman is somewhat simple,
  The better for a husband, were you wise;
  For those that marry fools, live Ladies lives.
  On with the Mask, I'll hear no more, he's rich;
  The fool's hid under Bushels.   95
LIVIA.   Not so hid neither;

But here's a foul great peece of him methinks;
What will he be, when he comes altogether?

Enter the WARD *with a Trap-stick, and* SORDIDO *his man.*

WARD.　Beat him?
　I beat him out o'th' field with his own Cat-stick,　　　100
　Yet gave him the first hand.
SORDIDO.　Oh strange!
WARD.　I did it,
　Then he set Jacks on me.
SORDIDO.　What, my Ladies Tailor?　　　105
WARD.　I, and I beat him too.
SORDIDO.　Nay that's no wonder,
　He's us'd to beating.
WARD.　Nay, I tickel'd him
　When I came once to my tippings!　　　110
SORDIDO.　Now you talk on 'em;
　There was a Poulterers wife made a great complaint of you last
　night to your Gardianer, that you struck a bump in her childes
　head, as big as an Egg.
WARD.　An Egg may prove a Chicken then in time; the Poulterers　115
　wife will get by't. When I am in game, I am furious; came my
　Mothers eyes in my way, I would not lose a fair end: No, were
　she alive, but with one tooth in her head, I should venture the
　striking out of that. I think of no body, when I am in play, I
　am so earnest. Coads-me, my Gardianer! Prethee lay up my Cat　120
　and Cat-stick safe.
SORDIDO.　Where Sir, i'th' Chimney-corner?
WARD.　Chimney Corner!
SORDIDO.　Yes Sir, your Cats are always safe i'th' Chimney
　Corner,
　Unless they burn their Coats.　　　125
WARD.　Marry, that I am afraid on!
SORDIDO.　Why, then I will bestow your Cat i'th' Gutter,
　And there she's safe I am sure.
WARD.　If I but live
　To keep a house, I'll make thee a great man,　　　130
　If meat and drink can do't. I can stoop gallantly,
　And pitch out when I list: I'm dog at a hole,

I mar'l my Guardianer do's not seek a wife for me;
I protest I'll have a bout with the Maids else,
Or contract my self at midnight to the Larder-woman,   135
In presence of a Fool, or a Sack-posset.

GUARDIANO.   Ward.

WARD.   I feel my self after any exercise
Horribly prone: Let me but ride, I'm lusty,
A Cock-horse straight y'faith.   140

GUARDIANO.   Why Ward, I say.

WARD.   I'll forswear eating Eggs in Moon-shine nights;
There's nev'r a one I eat, but turns into a Cock
In four and twenty hours; if my hot blood
Be not took down in time, sure 'twill crow shortly.   145

GUARDIANO.   Do you hear Sir? follow me, I must new School
you.

⟨*Exit.*⟩

WARD.   School me? I scorn that now, I am past schooling.
I am not so base to learn to write and read;
I was born to better fortunes in my Cradle.

Exit ⟨*followed by* SORDIDO.⟩

FABRITIO.   How do you like him Girl? this is your husband.   150
Like him, or like him not wench, you shall have him,
And you shall love him.

LIVIA.   Oh soft there Brother! though you be a Justice,
Your Warrant cannot be serv'd out of your liberty,
You may compel out of the power of Father,   155
Things meerly harsh to a Maids flesh and blood;
But when you come to love, there the soil alters;
Y'are in an other Country, where your Laws
Are no more set by, then the cacklings
Of Geese in *Romes* great Capitol.   160

FABRITIO.   Marry him she shall then,
Let her agree upon love afterwards.

Exit.

LIVIA.   You speak now Brother like an honest mortal
That walks upon th'earth with a staff;

You were up i'th' Clouds before, you'ld command love,   165
And so do most old folks that go without it.
My best and dearest Brother, I could dwell here;
There is not such another seat on earth,
Where all good parts better express themselves.
HIPPOLITO.   You'll make me blush anon.   170
LIVIA.   'Tis but like saying grace before a Feast then,
And that's most comely; thou art all a Feast,
And she that has thee, a most happy guest.
Prethee chear up that Neece with special Counsel.

⟨*Exit.*⟩

HIPPOLITO. ⟨*Aside.*⟩   I would 'twere fit to speak to her what I
would; but   571
'Twas not a thing ordain'd, Heaven has forbid it,
And 'tis most meet, that I should rather perish
Then the Decree Divine receive least blemish:
Feed inward you my sorrows, make no noise,
Consume me silent, let me be stark dead   180
Ere the world know I'm sick. You see my honesty,
If you befriend me, so.
ISABELLA.   Marry a Fool!
Can there be greater misery to a woman
That means to keep her days true to her husband,   185
And know no other man! so vertue wills it.
Why; how can I obey and honor him,
But I must needs commit Idolatry?
A Fool is but the Image of a man,
And that but ill made neither: Oh the heart-breakings   190
Of miserable Maids, where love's inforc'd!
The best condition is but bad enough;
When women have their choices, commonly
They do but buy their thraldoms, and bring great portions
To men to keep 'em in subjection,   195
As if a fearful prisoner should bribe
The Keeper to be good to him, yet lies in still,
And glad of a good usage, a good look
Sometimes by'r Lady; no misery surmounts a womans.
Men buy their slaves, but women buy their masters;   200

Yet honesty and love makes all this happy,
And next to Angels, the most blest estate.
That Providence, that h'as made ev'ry poyson
Good for some use, and sets four warring Elements
At peace in man, can make a harmony   205
In things that are most strange to humane reason.
Oh but this marriage! What are you sad too Uncle?
Faith then there's a whole houshold down together:
Where shall I go to seek my comfort now
When my best friend's distressed? what is't afflicts you Sir?   210

HIPPOLITO.   Faith nothing but one grief that will not leave me,
And now 'tis welcome; ev'ry man has something
To bring him to his end, and this will serve
Joyn'd with your fathers cruelty to you,
That helps it forward.   215

ISABELLA.   Oh be cheer'd sweet Uncle!
How long has't been upon you, I nev'r spi'd it:
What a dull sight have I, how long I pray Sir?

HIPPOLITO.   Since I first saw you Neece, and left *Bologna*.

ISABELLA.   And could you deal so unkindly with my heart,   220
To keep it up so long hid from my pitty?
Alas, how shall I trust your love hereafter?
Have we past through so many arguments,
And miss'd of that still, the most needful one?
Walk'd out whole nights together in discourses,   225
And the main point forgot? We are too blame both;
This is an obstinate wilful forgetfulness,
And faulty on both parts: Let's lose no time now,
Begin good Uncle, you that feel't; what is it?

HIPPOLITO.   You of all creatures Neece must never hear on't,   230
'Tis not a thing ordain'd for you to know.

ISABELLA.   Not I Sir! all my joys that word cuts off;
You made profession once you lov'd me best;
'Twas but profession!

HIPPOLITO.   Yes, I do't too truly,   235
And fear I shall be chid for't: Know the worst then:
I love thee dearlier then an Uncle can.

ISABELLA.   Why so you ever said, and I believ'd it.

HIPPOLITO. ⟨*Aside.*⟩   So simple is the goodness of her thoughts,

They understand not yet th'unhallowed language   240
Of a near sinner: I must yet be forced
(Though blushes be my venture) to come nearer.
⟨*To her.*⟩ As a man love's his wife, so love I thee.
ISABELLA.   What's that?
   Methought I heard ill news come toward me,   245
   Which commonly we understand too soon,
   Then over-quick at hearing, I'll prevent it,
   Though my joys fare the harder; welcome it:
   It shall nev'r come so near mine ear again.
   Farewel all friendly solaces and discourses,   250
   I'll learn to live without ye, for your dangers
   Are greater then your comforts; what's become
   Of truth in love, if such we cannot trust,
   When blood that should be love, is mix'd with lust.

                                                   Exit.

HIPPOLITO.   The worst can be but death, and let it come,   255
   He that lives joyless, ev'ry day's his doom.

                                                   Exit.

SCENE III

Enter LEANTIO *alone.*

LEANTIO.   Methinks I'm ev'n as dull now at departure,
   As men observe great Gallants the next day
   After a Revels; you shall see 'em look
   Much of my fashion, if you mark 'em well.
   'Tis ev'n a second Hell to part from pleasure,   5
   When man has got a smack on't: As many holidays
   Coming together makes your poor heads idle
   A great while after, and are said to stick
   Fast in their fingers ends; ev'n so does game
   In a new married couple for the time,   10
   It spoils all thrift, and indeed lies a Bed
   To invent all the new ways for great expences.

⟨*Enter*⟩ BRANCHA *and* MOTHER *above.*

See, and she be not got on purpose now
Into the Window to look after me,
I have no power to go now, and I should be hang'd: 15
Farewel all business, I desire no more
Then I see yonder; let the goods at Key
Look to themselves; why should I toil my youth out?
It is but begging two or three year sooner,
And stay with her continually; is't a match?   20
O fie, what a Religion have I leap'd into!
Get out again for shame, the man loves best
When his care's most, that shows his zeal to love.
Fondness is but the Idiot to Affection,
That plays at Hot-cockles with rich Merchants wives;   25
Good to make sport withal when the Chest's full,
And the long Ware house cracks. 'Tis time of day
For us to be more wise; 'tis early with us,
And if they lose the morning of their affairs,
They commonly lose the best part of the day,   30
Those that are wealthy, and have got enough:
'Tis after Sun-set with 'em, they may rest,
Grow fat with ease, banket, and toy and play,
When such as I enter the heat o'th' day,
And I'll do't cheerfully.   35
BRANCHA.   I perceive Sir
Y'are not gone yet, I have good hope you'll stay now.
LEANTIO.   Farewel, I must not.
BRANCHA.   Come, come, pray return
To morrow; adding but a little care more,   40
Will dispatch all as well; believe me 'twill Sir.
LEANTIO.   I could well wish my self where you would have me;
But love that's wanton, must be rul'd a while
By that that's careful, or all goes to ruine,
As fitting is a Government in Love,   45
As in a Kingdom; where 'tis all meer Lust,
'Tis like an insurrection in the people
That rais'd in Self-wil, wars against all Reason:
But Love that is respective for increase,
Is like a good King, that keeps all in peace.   50
Once more farewel.

BRANCHA.   But this one night I prethee.
LEANTIO.   Alas I'm in for twenty, if I stay,
   And then for forty more, I have such luck to flesh:
   I never bought a horse, but he bore double.   55
   If I stay any longer, I shall turn
   An everlasting spend-thrift; as you love
   To be maintain'd well, do not call me again,
   For then I shall not care which end goes forward:
   Again farewel to thee.   *Exit.* 60
BRANCHA.   Since it must, farewel too.
MOTHER.   'Faith daughter, y'are too blame, you take the course
   To make him an ill husband, troth you do,
   And that disease is catching, I can tell you,
   I, and soon taken by a yongmans blood,   65
   And that with little urging: Nay fie, see now,
   What cause have you to weep? would I had no more,
   That have liv'd threescore years; there were a cause
   And 'twere well thought on; trust me y'are too blame,
   His absence cannot last five days at utmost.   70
   Why should those tears be fetch'd forth? cannot love
   Be ev'n as well express'd in a good look,
   But it must see her face still in a Fountain,
   It shows like a Country Maid dressing her head
   By a dish of water: Come 'tis an old custom   75
   To weep for love.

Enter two or three BOYS, *and a* CITIZEN *or two, with an*
APPRENTICE.

BOYS.   Now they come, now they come.
SECOND BOY.   The Duke.
THIRD BOY.   The State.
CITIZEN.   How near Boy?   80
FIRST BOY.   I'th' next street Sir, hard at hand.
CITIZEN.   You sirra, get a standing for your Mistress,
   The best in all the City.
APPRENTICE.   I hav't for her Sir,
   'Twas a thing I provided for her over night,   85
   'Tis ready at her pleasure.
     W.B.W.—2*

CITIZEN.   Fetch her to't then, away Sir.

                                    ⟨*Exit* APPRENTICE.⟩

BRANCHA.   What's the meaning of this hurry,
    Can you tell Mother.
MOTHER.   What a memory   90
    Have I! I see by that years come upon me.
    Why 'tis a yearly custom and solemnity,
    Religiously observ'd by th'Duke and State
    To St. *Marks* Temple, the fifteenth of *April*.
    See if my dull brains had not quite forgot it,   95
    'Twas happily question'd of thee, I had gone down else,
    Sat like a drone below, and never thought on't.
    I would not to be ten years yonger again,
    That you had lost the sight; now you shall see
    Our Duke, a goodly Gentleman of his years.   100
BRANCHA.   Is he old then?
MOTHER.   About some fifty five.
BRANCHA.   That's no great age in man, he's then at best
    For wisdom, and for judgment.
MOTHER.   The Lord Cardinal   105
    His noble Brother, there's a comly Gentleman,
    And greater in devotion then in blood.
BRANCHA.   He's worthy to be mark'd.
MOTHER.   You shall behold
    All our cheif states of *Florence*, you came fortunately   110
    Against this solemn day.
BRANCHA.   I hope so always.

                                    Musick.

MOTHER.   I hear 'em near us now, do you stand easily?
BRANCHA.   Exceeding well, good Mother.
MOTHER.   Take this stool.   115
BRANCHA.   I need it not I thank you.
MOTHER.   Use your will then.

Enter in great solemnity six Knights
bare-headed, then two Cardinals, and then the
LORD CARDINAL, *then the* DUKE; *after*

him the States of Florence *by two and two,*
with varity of Musick and Song.   *Exit.*

MOTHER.   How like you Daughter?
BRANCHA.   'Tis a Noble State.
  Methinks my soul could dwell upon the reverence   120
  Of such a solemn and most worthy custom.
  Did not the Duke look up? me-thought he saw us.
MOTHER.   That's ev'ry one's conceit that sees a Duke,
  If he look stedfastly, he looks strait at them,
  When he perhaps, good careful Gentleman,   125
  Never mindes any; but the look he casts,
  Is at his own intentions, and his object
  Onely the publick good.
BRANCHA.   Most likely so.
MOTHER.   Come, come, we'll end this Argument below.   130

                              Exeunt.

ACT II

SCENE I

Enter HIPPOLITO, *and Lady* LIVIA *the Widow.*

LIVIA.   A Strange affection (Brother) when I think on't!
  I wonder how thou cam'st by't.
HIPPOLITO.   Ev'n as easily,
  As man comes by destruction, which oft-times
  He wears in his own bosom.   5
LIVIA.   Is the world
  So populous in Women, and Creation,
  So prodigal in Beauty, and so various?
  Yet do's love turn thy point to thine own blood?
  'Tis somewhat too unkindly; must thy eye   10
  Dwell evilly on the fairness of thy kinred,
  And seek not where it should? it is confin'd
  Now in a narrower prison then was made for't?
  It is allow'd a stranger, and where bounty
  Is made the great mans honor, 'tis ill husbandry   15

To spare, and servants shall have small thanks for't.
So he Heavens bounty seems to scorn and mock,
That spares free means, and spends of his own stock.
HIPPOLITO.   Never was mans misery so soon sow'd up,
  Counting how truly.   20
LIVIA.   Nay, I love you so,
  That I shall venture much to keep a change from you
  So fearful as this grief will bring upon you.
  Faith it even kills me, when I see you faint
  Under a reprehension, and I'll leave it,   25
  Though I know nothing can be better for you:
  Prethee (sweet Brother) let not passion waste
  The goodness of thy time, and of thy fortune:
  Thou keep'st the treasure of that life I love,
  As dearly as mine own; and if you think   30
  My former words too bitter, which were ministred
  By truth and zeal; 'tis but a hazarding
  Of grace and vertue, and I can bring forth
  As pleasant Fruits, as Sensualitie wishes
  In all her teeming longings: This I can do.   35
HIPPOLITO.   Oh nothing that can make my wishes perfect!
LIVIA.   I would that love of yours were pawn'd to't Brother,
  And as soon lost that way, as I could win.
  Sir I could give as shreud a lift to Chastity,
  As any she that wears a tongue in *Florence*.   40
  Sh'ad need be a good horse-woman, and sit fast,
  Whom my strong argument could not fling at last.
  Prethee take courage man; though I should counsel
  Another to despair, yet I am pitiful
  To thy afflictions, and will venture hard;   45
  I will not name for what, 'tis not handsom;
  Finde you the proof, and praise me.
HIPPOLITO.   Then I fear me,
  I shall not praise you in haste.
LIVIA.   This is the comfort,   50
  You are not the first (Brother) has attempted
  Things more forbidden, then this seems to be:
  I'll minister all Cordials now to you,
  Because I'll cheer you up Sir.

HIPPOLITO.   I am past hope.   55
LIVIA.   Love, thou shalt see me do a strange cure then,
　　As e'r was wrought on a disease so mortal,
　　And near akin to shame; when shall you see her?
HIPPOLITO.   Never in comfort more.
LIVIA.   Y'are so impatient too.   60
HIPPOLITO.   Will you believe—death, sh'has forsworn my
　　company,
　　And seal'd it with a blush.
LIVIA.   So, I perceive
　　All lies upon my hands then; well, the more glory
　　When the works finish'd—   65

Enter SERVANT.

　　How now Sir, the news!
SERVANT.   Madam, your Neece, the vertuous *Isabela*,
　　Is lighted now to see you.
LIVIA.   That's great fortune
　　Sir, your Stars bless; you simple, lead her in.   70

　　　　　　　　　　　　　　　　　　　　　　Exit SERVANT.

HIPPOLITO.   What's this to me?
LIVIA.   Your absence gentle Brother,
　　I must bestir my wits for you.
HIPPOLITO.   I, to great purpose.

　　　　　　　　　　　　　　　　　　　　　　Exit HIPPOLITO.

LIVIA.   Beshrew you, would I lov'd you not so well: 75
　　I'll go to Bed, and leave this deed undone:
　　I am the fondest where I once affect;
　　The carefull'st of their healths, and of their ease forsooth,
　　That I look still but slenderly to mine own.
　　I take a course to pity him so much now,   80
　　That I have none left for modesty and my self.
　　This 'tis to grow so liberal; y'have few sisters
　　That love their Brothers ease 'bove their own honesties:
　　But if you question my affections,
　　That will be found my fault.   85

　　　　　　　　II. I. 61 believe—] ~ₐ TNP.

Enter ISABELLA *the Neece.*

   Neece, your love's welcome.
   Alas what draws that paleness to thy cheeks,
   This inforc'd marriage towards?
ISABELLA.   It helps good Aunt
   Amongst some other griefs; but those I'll keep   90
   Lock'd up in modest silence; for they'r sorrows
   Would shame the Tongue, more then they grieve the thought.
LIVIA.   Indeed the Ward is simple.
ISABELLA.   Simple! that were well:
   Why one might make good shift with such a husband.   95
   But he's a fool entail'd, he halts down right in't.
LIVIA.   And knowing this, I hope 'tis at your choice
   To take or refuse Neece.
ISABELLA.   You see it is not.
   I loath him more then beauty can hate death   100
   Or age her spightful neighbor.
LIVIA.   Let't appear then.
ISABELLA.   How can I being born with that obedience,
   That must submit unto a fathers will?
   If he command, I must of force consent.   105
LIVIA.   Alas poor soul! be not offended prethee,
   If I set by the name of Neece a while,
   And bring in pity in a stranger fashion:
   It lies here in this Brest, would cross this match.
ISABELLA.   How, cross it Aunt?   110
LIVIA.   I, and give thee more liberty
   Then thou hast reason yet to apprehend.
ISABELLA.   Sweet Aunt, in goodness keep not hid from me
   What may befriend my life.
LIVIA.   Yes, yes, I must,   115
   When I return to reputation,
   And think upon the solemn Vow I made
   To your dead Mother, my most loving Sister;
   As long as I have her memory 'twixt mine eye lids,
   Look for no pity now.   120
ISABELLA.   Kinde, sweet, dear Aunt.
LIVIA.   No, 'twas a secret, I have took special care of,

Delivered by your Mother on her death bed,
That's nine years now, and I'll not part from't yet,
Though nev'r was fitter time, nor greater cause for't.   125
ISABELLA.   As you desire the praises of a Virgin—
LIVIA.   Good sorrow! I would do thee any kindness,
Not wronging Secrecy, or Reputation.
ISABELLA.   Neither of which (as I have hope of fruitfulness)
Shall receive wrong from me.   130
LIVIA.   Nay 'twould be your own wrong,
As much as any's, should it come to that once.
ISABELLA.   I need no better means to work perswasion then.
LIVIA.   Let it suffice, you may refuse this fool,
Or you may take him, as you see occasion   135
For your advantage; the best wits will do't;
Y'have liberty enough in your own will,
You cannot be inforc'd; there grows the flowre
If you could pick it out, makes whole life sweet to you.
That which you call your Fathers command's nothing;   140
Then your obedience must needs be as little:
If you can make shift here to taste your happiness,
Or pick out ought that likes you, much good do you:
You see your cheer, I'll make you no set dinner.
ISABELLA.   And trust me, I may starve for all the good   145
I can finde yet in this: Sweet Aunt, deal plainlier.
LIVIA.   Say I should trust you now upon an oath,
And give you in a secret that would start you,
How am I sure of you, in faith and silence?
ISABELLA.   Equal assurance may I finde in mercy,   150
As you for that in me.
LIVIA.   It shall suffice:
Then know, how ever custom h'as made good
For reputations sake, the names of Neece
And Aunt, 'twixt you and I, w'are nothing less.   155
ISABELLA.   How's that?
LIVIA.   I told you I should start your blood.
You are no more alli'd to any of us,
Save what the curtesie of opinion casts

<hr/>

129 fruitfulness] DILKE; fruit-/ness TNP.

Upon your Mothers memory, and your name,   160
Then the meer'st stranger is, or one begot
At *Naples*, when the husband lies at *Rome*;
There's so much oddes betwixt us. Since your knowledge
Wish'd more instruction, and I have your oath
In pledge for silence; it makes me talk the freelier.   165
Did never the report of that fam'd *Spaniard*,
Marquess of *Coria*, since your time was ripe
For understanding, fill your ear with wonder?

ISABELLA.   Yes, what of him? I have heard his deeds of honor
Often related when we liv'd in *Naples*.   170

LIVIA.   You heard the praises of your Father then.

ISABELLA.   My Father!

LIVIA.   That was he: But all the business
So carefully and so discreetly carried,
That Fame receiv'd no spot by't, not a blemish;   175
Your Mother was so wary to her end,
None knew it, but her Conscience, and her friend,
Till penitent confession made it mine,
And now my pity, yours: It had been long else,
And I hope care and love alike in you,   180
Made good by oath, will see it take no wrong now:
How weak his commands now, whom you call Father?
How vain all his inforcements, your obedience?
And what a largeness in your will and liberty,
To take, or to reject, or to do both?   185
For fools will serve to father wisemens children:
All this y'have time to think on. O my Wench!
Nothing o'rthrows our Sex but indiscretion,
We might do well else of a brittle people,
As any under the great Canopy: 190
I pray forget not but to call me Aunt still;
Take heed of that, it may be mark'd in time else,
But keep your thoughts to your self, from all the world,
Kinred, or dearest friend, nay, I entreat you,
From him that all this while you have call'd Uncle;   195
And though you love him dearly, as I know
His deserts claim as much ev'n from a stranger,
Yet let not him know this, I prethee do not,

As ever thou hast hope of second pity,
If thou shouldst stand in need on't, do not do't.   200
ISABELLA.   Believe my oath, I will not.
    LIVIA.   Why well said:
    ⟨*Aside.*⟩ Who shows more craft t'undo a Maidenhead,
    I'll resign my part to her;

Enter HIPPOLITO.

    ⟨*Aside to him.*⟩ She's thine own, go.   205

                                                                      Exit.

HIPPOLITO.   Alas, fair flattery cannot cure my sorrows!
ISABELLA. ⟨*Aside*⟩   Have I past so much time in ignorance,
    And never had the means to know my self
    Till this blest hour? Thanks to her vertuous pity
    That brought it now to light; would I had known it   210
    But one day sooner, he had then receiv'd
    In favors, what (poor Gentleman) he took
    In bitter words; a slight and harsh reward
    For one of his deserts.
HIPPOLITO. ⟨*Aside*⟩   There seems to me now   215
    More anger and distraction in her looks.
    I'm gone, I'll not endure a second storm;
    The memory of the first, is not past yet.
ISABELLA.   Are you return'd, you comforts of my life?
    In this mans presence, I will keep you fast now,   220
    And sooner part eternally from the world,
    Then my good joys in you: Prethee forgive me,
    I did but chide in jest; the best loves use it
    Sometimes, it sets an edge upon affection:
    When we invite our best friends to a feast,   225
    'Tis not all sweet-meats that we set before them,
    There's somewhat sharp and salt, both to whet Appetite,
    And make 'em taste their Wine well: So methinks
    After a friendly, sharpe and savory chiding,
    A kiss tastes wondrous well, and full o'th' Grape.   230

                                                      ⟨*Kisses him.*⟩

How think'st thou, do'st not?

HIPPOLITO.   'Tis so excellent,
  I know not how to praise it, what to say too't.
ISABELLA.   This marriage shall go forward.
HIPPOLITO.   With the Ward,   235
  Are you in earnest?
ISABELLA.   'Twould be ill for us else.
HIPPOLITO. ⟨*Aside.*⟩   For us? how means she that?
ISABELLA.   Troth I begin
  To be so well methinks, within this hour,   240
  For all this match able to kill ones heart:
  Nothing can pull me down now, should my Father
  Provide a worse fool yet (which I should think
  Were a hard thing to compass) I'd have him either;
  The worse the better, none can come amiss now,   245
  If he want wit enough: So Discretion love me,
  Desert and Judgment, I have content sufficient.
  She that comes once to be a house-keeper,
  Must not look every day to fare well Sir,
  Like a yong waiting Gentlewoman in service,   250
  For she feeds commonly as her Lady does;
  No good bit passes her, but she gets a taste on't;
  But when she comes to keep house for her self,
  She's glad of some choice Cates then once a week,
  Or twice at most, and glad if she can get 'em: 255
  So must Affection learn to fare with thankfulness.
  Pray make your Love no stranger Sir, that's all,
  ⟨*Aside.*⟩ Though you be one your self, and know not on't,
  And I have sworn you must not.

                                           Exit.

HIPPOLITO.   This is beyond me!   260
  Never came joys so unexpectedly
  To meet desires in man; how came she thus?
  What has she done to her can any tell?
  'Tis beyond Sorcery this, Drugs, or Love-powders;
  Some Art that has no name sure, strange to me   265
  Of all the wonders I ere met withal
  Throughout my ten years travels, but I'm thankful for't.
  This marriage now must of necessity forward;

It is the onely vail Wit can devise
To keep our acts hid from sin-peircing eyes.   270

Exit.

SCENE II

Enter GUARDIANO *and* LIVIA.

LIVIA.   How Sir, a Gentlewoman, so yong, so fair,
  As you set forth, spi'd from the Widows window!
GUARDIANO.   Shee!
LIVIA.   Our Sunday-dinner woman?
GUARDIANO.   And thursday Supper-woman, the same still.   5
  I know not how she came by her, but I'll swear
  She's the prime gallant for a face, in *Florence*;
  And no doubt other parts follow their Leader:
  The Duke himself first spi'd her at the window,
  Then in a rapture, as if admiration   10
  Were poor when it were single, beck'ned me,
  And pointed to the wonder warily,
  As one that fear'd she would draw in her splendor
  Too soon, if too much gaz'd at: I nev'r knew him
  So infinitely taken with a woman,   15
  Nor can I blame his Appetite, or tax
  His Raptures of slight folly, she's a Creature
  Able to draw a State from serious business,
  And make it their best peece to do her service:
  What course shall we devise? h'as spoke twice now.   20
LIVIA.   Twice?
GUARDIANO.   'Tis beyond your apprehension.
  How strangly that one look has catch'd his heart:
  'Twould prove but too much worth in wealth and favor
  To those should work his peace.   25
LIVIA.   And if I do't not,
  Or at least come as near it, (if your Art
  Will take a little pains, and second me)
  As any wench in *Florence* of my standing,
  I'll quite give o'r, and shut up shop in cunning.   30
GUARDIANO.   'Tis for the Duke, and if I fail your purpose,

All means to come, by riches or advancement,
Miss me, and skip me over.
LIVIA.   Let the old woman then
Be sent for with all speed, then I'll begin.   35
GUARDIANO.   A good conclusion follow, and a sweet one
After this stale beginning with old ware. Within there!

Enter SERVANT.

SERVANT.   Sir, do you call?
GUARDIANO.   Come near, list hither.

⟨*Speaks to him aside.*⟩

LIVIA.   I long my self to see this absolute Creature,   40
That wins the heart of love, and praise so much.
GUARDIANO.   Go Sir, make haste.
LIVIA.   Say I entreat her company;
Do you hear Sir?
SERVANT.   Yes Madam.   45

Exit.

LIVIA.   That brings her quickly.
GUARDIANO.   I would 'twere done, the Duke waits the good
hour,
And I wait the good Fortune that may spring from't.
I have had a lucky hand these fifteen year
At such Court Passage with three Dice in a Dish.   50

Enter FABRITIO.

Seignior *Fabritio*!
FABRITIO.   Oh Sir, I bring an alteration in my mouth now.
GUARDIANO. ⟨*Aside.*⟩   An alteration! no wise Speech I hope;
He means not to talk wisely, does he trow?
⟨*To him.*⟩ Good! what's the change I pray Sir?   55
FABRITIO.   A new change.
GUARDIANO.   Another yet! faith there's enough already.
FABRITIO.   My daughter loves him now.
GUARDIANO.   What does she Sir?
FABRITIO.   Affects him beyond thought, who but the Ward
forsooth!   60
No talk but of the Ward; she would have him

To chuse 'bove all the men she ever saw.
My Will goes not so fast, as her consent now;
Her duty gets before my command still.
GUARDIANO.   Why then Sir, if you'll have me speak my
     thoughts,   65
I smell 'twill be a match.
FABRITIO.   I, and a sweet yong couple,
If I have any judgment.
GUARDIANO. ⟨*Aside.*⟩   Faith that's little:
     ⟨*To him.*⟩ Let her be sent to morrow before noon,   70
And handsomly trick'd up; for 'bout that time
I mean to bring her in, and tender her to him.
FABRITIO.   I warrant you for handsom, I will see
Her things laid ready, every one in order,
And have some part of her trick'd up to night.   75
GUARDIANO.   Why well said.
FABRITIO.   'Twas a use her Mother had,
When she was invited to an early wedding;
She'ld dress her head o'r night, spunge up her self,
And give her neck three lathers.   80
GUARDIANO. ⟨*Aside.*⟩   Ne'r a halter?
FABRITIO.   On with her chain of Pearl, her ruby Bracelets,
Lay ready all her tricks, and Jiggam-bobs.
GUARDIANO.   So must your daughter.
FABRITIO.   I'll about it straight Sir.   85

                                        Exit FABRITIO.

LIVIA.   How he sweats in the foolish zeal of Fatherhood,
After six ounces an hour, and seems
To toil as much as if his cares were wise ones!
GUARDIANO.   Y'have let his folly blood in the right vain, Lady.
LIVIA.   And here comes his sweet Son-in-law that shall be;   90
They're both alli'd in wit before the marriage;
What will they be hereafter, when they are neerer?
Yet they can go no further then the Fool:
There's the worlds end in both of 'em.

Enter WARD *and* SORDIDO, *one with a Shittlecock
the other a Battledoor.*

GUARDIANO.   Now yong heir.   95
WARD.   What's the next business after Shittlecock now?
GUARDIANO.   To morrow you shall see the Gentlewoman
  Must be your wife.
WARD.   There's ev'n an other thing too
  Must be kept up with a pair of Battledoors.   100
  My wife! what can she do?
GUARDIANO.   Nay that's a question you should ask your self,
  Ward,
  When y'are alone together.
WARD.   That's as I list.
  A wife's to be ask'd any where I hope;   105
  I'll ask her in a Congregation, if I have a minde to't, and so save
  a Licence: My Guardiner has no more wit then an Herb-woman,
  that sells away all her sweet Herbs and Nose-gays, and keeps a
  stinking breath for her own Pottage.
SORDIDO.   Let me be at the chusing of your beloved,   110
  If you desire a woman of good parts.
WARD.   Thou shalt sweet *Sordido*.
SORDIDO.   I have a plaguy ghess, let me alone to see what she is;
  if I but look upon her—why, I know all the faults to a hair, that
  you may refuse her for.   115
WARD.   Do'st thou! I prethee let me hear 'em *Sordido*.
SORDIDO.   Well, mark 'em then; I have 'em all in rime.
  The wife your Guardiner ought to tender,
  Should be pretty, straight and slender;
  Her hair not short, her foot not long,   120
  Her hand not huge, nor too too loud her tongue:
  No pearl in eye, nor ruby in her nose,
  No burn or cut, but what the Catalogue shows.
  She must have teeth, and that no black ones,
  And kiss most sweet when she does smack once: 125
  Her skin must be both white and plump,
  Her body straight, not hopper rumpt,
  Or wriggle side-ways like a Crab;
  She must be neither Slut nor Drab,

II. II. 114 why] way TNP. "*Why*" *is a favourite Middleton exclamation, but he
does not use* "*way*" *like this.*
120 Her] DILKE; Heir TNP.

Nor go too splay-foot with her shooes,   130
To make her Smock lick up the dews.
And two things more, which I forgot to tell ye
She neither must have bump in back, nor belly.
These are the faults that will not make her pass.
WARD.   And if I spie not these, I am a rank Ass.   135
SORDIDO.   Nay more; by right Sir, you should see her naked,
For that's the ancient order.
WARD.   See her naked?
That were good sport y'faith: I'll have the Books turn'd over;
And if I finde her naked on Record,   140
She shall not have a rag on: But stay, stay,
How if she should desire to see me so too,
I were in a sweet case then, such a fowl skin.
SORDIDO.   But y'have a clean shirt, and that makes amends Sir.
WARD.   I will not see her naked for that trick though.   145

                                                            Exit.

SORDIDO.   Then take her with all faults, with her cloaths on!
And they may hide a number with a bum-roll.
'Faith chusing of a Wench in a huge Farthingale,
Is like the buying of ware under a great Pent-house:
What with the deceit of one,   150
And the false light of th'other, mark my Speeches,
He may have a diseas'd Wench in's Bed,
And rotten stuff in's Breeches.

                                                            Exit.

GUARDIANO.   It may take handsomly.
LIVIA.   I see small hind'rance: 155
How now, so soon return'd?

Enter MOTHER ⟨*shown in by* SERVANT⟩.

GUARDIANO.   She's come.

                                            ⟨*Exit* SERVANT.⟩

LIVIA.   That's well.
Widdow, come, come, I have a great quarrel to you,
Faith I must chide you, that you must be sent for!   160

You make your self so strange, never come at us;
And yet so neer a neighbor, and so unkinde;
Troth y'are too blame, you cannot be more welcome
To any house in *Florence*, that I'll tell you.

MOTHER.   My thanks must needs acknowledge so much Madam.   165

LIVIA.   How can you be so strange then? I sit here
Sometime whole days together without company,
When business draws this Gentleman from home,
And should be happy in society,
Which I so well affect, as that of yours.   170
I know y'are alone too; why should not we
Like two kinde neighbors, then supply the wants
Of one another, having tongue discourse,
Experience in the world, and such kinde helps
To laugh down time, and meet age merrily?   175

MOTHER.   Age (Madam) you speak mirth; 'tis at my door,
But a long journey from your Ladiship yet.

LIVIA.   My faith I'm nine and thirty, ev'ry stroak Wench,
And 'tis a general observation
'Mongst Knights, Wives, or Widows, we accompt   180
Our selves then old, when yong mens eyes leave looking at's:
'Tis a true rule amongst us, and ne'r fail'd yet
In any but in one, that I remember;
Indeed she had a friend at nine and forty;
Marry she paid well for him, and in th'end   185
He kept a Quean or two with her own money,
That robb'd her of her plate, and cut her throat.

MOTHER.   She had her punishment in this world (Madam)
And a fair warning to all other women,
That they live chaste at fifty.   190

LIVIA.   I, or never Wench:
Come, now I have thy company I'll not part with't
Till after supper.

MOTHER.   Yes, I must crave pardon (Madam).

---

175 merrily] DILKE; meerly TNP. *In Middleton's hand, an undotted* i *is easily mistaken for an* e; *if he wrote* merilie, *the scribe may have misread it as* merelie, *and transcribed it (in accordance with his own spelling-habits) as* meerly. *The spelling* merrily *is one that could have been expected in* TNP *if the word had been correctly interpreted.*

LIVIA.   I swear you shall stay supper; we have no strangers,
  woman,   195
    None but my sojourners and I; this Gentleman
    And the yong heir his Ward; you know our company.
MOTHER.   Some other time, I will make bold with you Madam.
GUARDIANO.   Nay pray stay Widow.
LIVIA.   'Faith, she shall not go;   20c
    Do you think I'll be forsworn?

                                        Table and Chess.

MOTHER.   'Tis a great while
    Till supper time; I'll take my leave then now (Madam)
    And come again i'th' evening, since your Ladiship
    Will have it so.   205
LIVIA.   I'th' evening! by my troth Wench,
    I'll keep you while I have you; you have great business sure,
    To sit alone at home; I wonder strangely
    What pleasure you take in't! were't to me now
    I should be ever at one Neighbours house   210
    Or other all day long; having no charge,
    Or none to chide you, if you go, or stay,
    Who may live merrier, I, or more at hearts-ease?
    Come, we'll to Chess, or Draughts; there are an hundred tricks
    To drive out time till Supper, never fear't Wench.   215
MOTHER.   I'll but make one step home, and return straight
    (Madam).
LIVIA.   Come, I'll not trust you; you use more excuses
    To your kinde friends then ever I knew any.
    What business can you have, if you be sure
    Y'have lock'd the doors? and that being all you have   22c
    I know y'are careful on't: one afternoon
    So much to spend here! say I should entreat you now
    To lie a night or two, or a week with me,
    Or leave your own house for a moneth together,
    It were a kindness that long Neighborhood   225
    And friendship might well hope to prevail in:
    Would you deny such a request y'faith,
    Speak truth, and freely.
MOTHER.   I were then uncivil Madam.

LIVIA.   Go too then, set your men; we'll have whole nights   230
    Of mirth together, ere we be much older, Wench.
MOTHER. ⟨*Aside.*⟩   As good now tell her then, for she will know't;
    I have always found her a most friendly Lady.
LIVIA.   Why Widow, where's your minde?
MOTHER.   Troth ev'n at home Madam.   235
    To tell you truth, I left a Gentlewoman
    Ev'n sitting all alone, which is uncomfortable,
    Especially to yong bloods.
LIVIA.   Another excuse!
MOTHER.   No, as I hope for health, Madam, that's a truth,   240
    Please you to send and see.
LIVIA.   What Gentlewoman? pish.
MOTHER.   Wife to my son indeed, but not known (Madam)
    To any but your self.
LIVIA.   Now I beshrew you,   245
    Could you be so unkinde to her and me,
    To come and not bring her? Faith 'tis not friendly.
MOTHER.   I fear'd to be too bold.
LIVIA.   Too bold? Oh what's become
    Of the true hearty love was wont to be   250
    'Mongst Neighbors in old time?
MOTHER.   And she's a stranger (Madam).
LIVIA.   The more should be her welcome; when is courtesie
    In better practice, then when 'tis employ'd
    In entertaining strangers? I could chide y'Faith.   255
    Leave her behinde, poor Gentlewoman, alone too!
    Make some amends, and send for her betimes, go.
MOTHER.   Please you command one of your Servants Madam.
LIVIA.   Within there.

Enter SERVANT.

SERVANT.   Madam.   260
LIVIA.   Attend the Gentlewoman.
MOTHER. ⟨*Aside.*⟩   It must be carried wondrous privately
    From my Sons knowledge, he'll break out in storms else.
    Hark you Sir.

⟨*Speaks aside to* SERVANT.⟩

LIVIA.   Now comes in the heat of your part.   265
GUARDIANO.   True, I know it (Lady) and if I be out,
  May the Duke banish me from all employments,
  Wanton, or serious.

                                    ⟨*Exit* SERVANT.⟩

LIVIA.   So, have you sent Widow?
MOTHER.   Yes (Madam) he's almost at home by this.   270
LIVIA.   And 'faith let me entreat you, that hence forward,
  All such unkinde faults may be swept from friendship,
  Which does but dim the lustre; and think thus much
  It is a wrong to me, that have ability
  To bid friends welcome, when you keep 'em from me,   275
  You cannot set greater dishonor neer me;
  For Bounty is the credit and the glory
  Of those that have enough: I see y'are sorry,
  And the good mends is made by't.
MOTHER.   Here she's Madam.   280
Enter BRANCHA, *and* SERVANT.

                                    ⟨*Exit* SERVANT.⟩

BRANCHA. ⟨*Aside.*⟩   I wonder how she comes to send for me now?
LIVIA.   Gentlewoman, y'are most welcome, trust me y'are,
  As curtesie can make one, or respect
  Due to the presence of you.
BRANCHA.   I give you thanks, Lady.   285
LIVIA.   I heard you were alone, and 't had appear'd
  An ill condition in me, though I knew you not,
  Nor ever saw you, (yet humanity
  Thinks ev'ry case her own) to have kept your company
  Here from you, and left you all solitary: 290
  I rather ventur'd upon boldness then
  As the least fault, and wish'd your presence here;
  A thing most happily motion'd of that Gentleman,
  Whom I request you, for his care and pity
  To honor and reward with your acquaintance,   295
  A Gentleman that Ladies rights stands for,
  That's his profession.
BRANCHA.   'Tis a noble one, and honors my acquaintance.

GUARDIANO.   All my intentions are servants to such
  Mistresses.

BRANCHA.   'Tis your modesty   300
  It seems, that makes your deserts speak so low Sir.

LIVIA.   Come Widow, look you Lady, here's our business;
  Are we not well employ'd think you! an old quarrel
  Between us, that will never be at an end.

BRANCHA.   No, and methinks there's men enough to part you
  (Lady).   305

LIVIA.   Ho! but they set us on, let us come off
  As well as we can, poor souls, men care no farther.
  I pray sit down forsooth, if you have the patience
  To look upon two weak and tedious Gamesters.

GUARDIANO.   Faith Madam, set these by till evening,   310
  You'll have enough on't then; the Gentlewoman
  Being a stranger, would take more delight
  To see your rooms and pictures.

LIVIA.   Marry, good Sir,
  And well remembred, I beseech you shew 'em her;   315
  That will beguile time well; pray heartily do Sir,
  I'll do as much for you; here take these keys,
  Shew her the Monument too, and that's a thing
  Every one sees not; you can witness that Widow.

MOTHER.   And that's worth sight indeed, Madam.   320

BRANCHA.   Kinde Lady,
  I fear I came to be a trouble to you.

LIVIA.   Oh nothing less forsooth.

BRANCHA.   And to this courteous Gentleman,
  That wears a kindness in his Brest so noble   325
  And bounteous to the welcome of a stranger.

GUARDIANO.   If you but give acceptance to my service,
  You do the greatest grace and honor to me
  That curtesie can merit.

BRANCHA.   I were too blame else,   330
  And out of fashion much. I pray you lead Sir.

LIVIA.   After a game or two, w'are for you Gentlefolks.

GUARDIANO.   We wish no better seconds in Society
  Then your discourses, Madam, and your partners there.

MOTHER.   I thank your praise, I listen'd to you Sir;   335

Though when you spoke, there came a paltry Rook
Full in my way, and choaks up all my game.

Exit GUARDIANO *and* BRANCHA.

LIVIA.   Alas poor Widow, I shall be too hard for thee.
MOTHER.   Y'are cunning at the game, I'll be sworn (Madam).
LIVIA.   It will be found so, ere I give you over: 340
She that can place her man well—
MOTHER.   As you do (Madam).
LIVIA.   As I shall (Wench) can never lose her game;
Nay, nay, the black King's mine.
MOTHER.   Cry you mercy (Madam.)   345
LIVIA.   And this my Queen.
MOTHER.   I see't now.
LIVIA.   Here's a Duke
Will strike a sure stroke for the game anon;
Your pawn cannot come back to relieve it self.   350
MOTHER.   I know that (Madam.)
LIVIA.   You play well the whilst;
How she belies her skill! I hold two duckats,
I give you Check and Mate to your white King:
Simplicity it self, your Saintish King there.   355
MOTHER.   Well, ere now Lady
I have seen the fall of Subtilty: Jest on.
LIVIA.   I but Simplicitie receives two for one.
MOTHER.   What remedy but patience!

Enter above GUARDIANO *and* BRANCHA.

BRANCHA.   Trust me Sir,   360
Mine eye nev'r met with fairer Ornaments.
GUARDIANO.   Nay, livelier, I'm perswaded, neither *Florence*
Nor *Venice* can produce.
BRANCHA.   Sir, my opinion
Takes your part highly.   365
GUARDIANO.   There's a better peece
Yet then all these.

⟨*Enter*⟩ DUKE *above.*

BRANCHA.   Not possible Sir!
GUARDIANO.   Believe it
   You'll say so when you see't: Turn but your eye now   370
   Y'are upon't presently.

                                                   Exit.

BRANCHA.   Oh Sir.
DUKE.   He's gone Beauty!
   Pish, look not after him: He's but a vapor,
   That when the Sun appears, is seen no more.   375
BRANCHA.   Oh treachery to honor!
DUKE.   Prethee tremble not;
   I feel thy brest shake like a Turtle panting
   Under a loving hand that makes much on't;
   Why art so fearful? as I'm friend to brightness,   380
   There's nothing but respect and honor near thee:
   You know me, you have seen me; here's a heart
   Can witness I have seen thee.
BRANCHA.   The more's my danger.
DUKE.   The more's thy happiness: Pish strive not Sweet;   385
   This strength were excellent employ'd in love now,
   But here 'tis spent amiss; strive not to seek
   Thy liberty, and keep me still in prison.
   'Yfaith you shall not out, till I'm releast now;
   We'll be both freed together, or stay still by't;   390
   So is captivity pleasant.
BRANCHA.   Oh my Lord.
DUKE.   I am not here in vain; have but the leisure
   To think on that, and thou'lt be soon resolv'd:
   The lifting of thy voice, is but like one   395
   That does exalt his enemy, who proving high,
   Lays all the plots to confound him that rais'd him.
   Take warning I beseech thee; thou seem'st to me
   A creature so compos'd of gentleness,
   And delicate meekness; such as bless the faces   400
   Of figures that are drawn for Goddesses,
   And makes Art proud to look upon her work:
   I should be sorry the least force should lay
   An unkinde touch upon thee.

BRANCHA.   Oh my extremity!   405
   My Lord, what seek you?
DUKE.   Love.
BRANCHA.   'Tis gone already,
   I have a husband.
DUKE.   That's a single comfort,   410
   Take a friend to him.
BRANCHA.   That's a double mischeif,
   Or else there's no Religion.
DUKE.   Do not tremble
   At fears of thine own making.   415
BRANCHA.   Nor great Lord,
   Make me not bold with death and deeds of ruine
   Because they fear not you; me they must fright;
   Then am I best in health: Should thunder speak,
   And none regard it, it had lost the name,   420
   And were as good be still. I'm not like those
   That take their soundest sleeps in greatest tempests,
   Then wake I most, the weather fearfullest,
   And call for strength to vertue.
DUKE.   Sure I think   425
   Thou know'st the way to please me. I affect
   A passionate pleading, 'bove an easie yeilding,
   But never pitied any, they deserve none
   That will not pity me: I can command,
   Think upon that; yet if thou truly knewest   430
   The infinite pleasure my affection takes
   In gentle, fair entreatings, when loves businesses
   Are carried curteously 'twixt heart and heart,
   You'ld make more haste to please me.
BRANCHA.   Why should you seek Sir,   435
   To take away that you can never give?
DUKE.   But I give better in exchange; wealth, honor:
   She that is fortunate in a Dukes favor,
   Lights on a Tree that bears all womens wishes:
   If your own Mother saw you pluck fruit there,   440
   She would commend your wit, and praise the time
   Of your Nativity, take hold of glory.
   Do not I know y'have cast away your life

Upon necessities, means meerly doubtful
To keep you in indifferent health and fashion.   445
(A thing I heard too lately, and soon pitied)
And can you be so much your Beauties enemy,
To kiss away a moneth or two in wedlock,
And weep whole years in wants for ever after?
Come play the wise wench, and provide for ever;   450
Let storms come when they list, they finde thee shelter'd:
Should any doubt arise, let nothing trouble thee;
Put trust in our love for the managing
Of all to thy hearts peace. We'll walk together,
And shew a thankful joy for both our fortunes.   455

Exit ⟨DUKE *and* BRANCHA⟩ *above.*

LIVIA.   Did not I say my Duke would fetch you over (Widow)?
MOTHER.   I think you spoke in earnest when you said it
   (Madam).
LIVIA.   And my black King makes all the haste he can too.
MOTHER.   Well (Madam) we may meet with him in time yet.
LIVIA.   I have given thee blinde mate twice.   460
MOTHER.   You may see (Madam)
   My eyes begin to fail.
LIVIA.   I'll swear they do, Wench.

Enter GUARDIANO.

GUARDIANO. ⟨*Aside.*⟩   I can but smile as often as I think on't,
How prettily the poor fool was beguild: 465
How unexpectedly; it's a witty age,
Never were finer snares for womens honesties
Then are devis'd in these days; no Spiders web
Made of a daintier thred, then are now practis'd
To catch loves flesh-flie by the silver wing: 470
Yet to prepare her stomach by degrees
To *Cupids* feast, because I saw 'twas quezy,
I shew'd her naked pictures by the way;
A bit to stay the appetite. Well, Advancement!
I venture hard to finde thee; if thou com'st   475
With a greater title set upon thy Crest,

          450 wise] DILKE; wife TNP.

I'll take that first cross patiently, and wait
Until some other comes greater then that.
I'll endure all.

LIVIA.   The game's ev'n at the best now; you may see Widow   480
How all things draw to an end.

MOTHER.   Ev'n so do I Madam.

LIVIA.   I pray take some of your neighbors along with you.

MOTHER.   They must be those are almost twice your years then,
If they be chose fit matches for my time, Madam.   485

LIVIA.   Has not my Duke bestir'd himself?

MOTHER.   Yes faith Madam; h'as done me all the mischief in this
Game.

LIVIA.   H'as shew'd himself in's kinde.

MOTHER.   In's kinde, call you it?
I may swear that.   490

LIVIA.   Yes faith, and keep your oath.

GUARDIANO. ⟨*Aside.*⟩   Hark, list, there's some body coming
down; 'tis she.

Enter BRANCHA.

BRANCHA. ⟨*Aside.*⟩   Now bless me from a blasting; I saw that
now,
Fearful for any womans eye to look on:
Infectious mists, and mill-dews hang at's eyes: 495
The weather of a doomsday dwells upon him.
Yet since mine honors Leprous, why should I
Preserve that fair that caus'd the Leprosie?
Come poyson all at once: ⟨*To him.*⟩ Thou in whose baseness
The bane of Vertue broods, I'm bound in Soul   500
Eternally to curse thy smooth brow'd treachery,
That wore the fair vail of a friendly welcome,
And I a stranger; think upon't, 'tis worth it.
Murders pil'd up upon a guilty spirit,
At his last breath will not lie heavier   505
Then this betraying Act upon thy Conscience:
Beware of offring the first-fruits to sin;
His weight is deadly, who commits with strumpets,

---

497 why] DILKE; who TNP. *Foul case or muscular error: o and y were in adjacent boxes.*

After they have been abas'd, and made for use;
If they offend to th'death, as wise men know,   510
How much more they then that first make 'em so?
I give thee that to feed on; I'm made bold now,
I thank thy treachery; sin and I'm acquainted,
No couple greater; and I'm like that great one,
Who making politick use of a base villain,   515
He likes the Treason well, but hates the Traytor;
So I hate thee slave.
GUARDIANO.   Well, so the Duke love me,
I fare not much amiss then; two great Feasts
Do seldom come together in one day;   520
We must not look for 'em.
BRANCHA.   What at it still Mother?
MOTHER.   You see we sit by't; are you so soon return'd?
LIVIA. ⟨*Aside.*⟩   So lively, and so chearful, a good sign that.
MOTHER.   You have not seen all since sure?   525
BRANCHA.   That have I Mother,
The Monument and all: I'm so beholding
To this kinde, honest, curteous Gentleman,
You'ld little think it (Mother) show'd me all,
Had me from place to place, so fashionably;   530
The kindness of some people, how't exceeds?
'Faith, I have seen that I little thought to see,
I'th' morning when I rose.
MOTHER.   Nay, so I told you
Before you saw't, it would prove worth your sight.   535
I give you great thanks for my daughter Sir,
And all your kindness towards her.
GUARDIANO.   O good Widow!
Much good may do her; ⟨*Aside.*⟩ forty weeks hence, y'faith.

Enter SERVANT.

LIVIA.   Now Sir.   540
SERVANT.   May't please you Madam to walk in,
Supper's upon the Table?
LIVIA.   Yes, we come;
Wilt please you Gentlewoman?
BRANCHA.   Thanks vertuous Lady,   545

(Y'are a damn'd Baud) I'll follow you forsooth,
   Pray take my Mother in, an old Ass go with you;
   This Gentleman and I vow not to part.
LIVIA.   Then get you both before.
BRANCHA.   There lies his art.   550
LIVIA.   Widow I'll follow you;

                         Exeunt ⟨all except LIVIA⟩.

                    is't so, Damn'd Baud?
   Are you so bitter? 'Tis but want of use;
   Her tender modesty is Sea-sick a little,
   Being not accustom'd to the breaking billow
   Of Womans wavering Faith, blown with temptations.   555
   'Tis but a qualm of honor, 'twill away,
   A little bitter for the time, but lasts not.
   Sin tastes at the first draught like Worm-wood Water,
   But drunk again, 'tis *Nectar* ever after.

                                              Exit.

                         ACT III

                         SCENE I

                    Enter MOTHER.

MOTHER.   I Would my Son would either keep at home,
   Or I were in my grave; she was but one day abroad, but ever since
   She's grown so cutted, there's no speaking to her:
   Whether the sight of great chear at my Ladies,
   And such mean fare at home, work discontent in her,   5
   I know not; but I'm sure she's strangely alter'd.
   I'll nev'r keep daughter-in-law i'th' house with me
   Again, if I had an hundred: When read I of any
   That agreed long together, but she and her mother
   Fell out in the first quarter! nay, sometime   10
   A grudging or a scolding the first week by'r Lady;
   So takes the new disease methinks in my house;
            III. I. II or] BULLEN; of TNP.

I'm weary of my part, there's nothing likes her;
I know not how to please her, here a-late;
And here she comes.   15

Enter BRANCHA.

BRANCHA.   This is the strangest house
For all defects, as ever Gentlewoman
Made shift withal, to pass away her love in!
Why is there not a Cushion-cloth of Drawn work,
Or some fair Cut-work pin'd up in my Bed-chamber.   20
A silver and gilt casting-Bottle hung by't?
Nay, since I am content to be so kinde to you,
To spare you for a silver Bason and Ewre,
Which one of my fashion looks for of duty;
She's never offered under, where she sleeps—   25
MOTHER.   She talks of things here my whole state's not worth.
BRANCHA.   Never a green silk quilt is there i'th' house Mother,
To cast upon my Bed?
MOTHER.   No by troth is there,
Nor orange tawny neither.   30
BRANCHA.   Here's a house
For a yong Gentlewoman to be got with childe in.
MOTHER.   Yes, simple though you make it, there has been three
Got in a year in't, since you move me to't;
And all as sweet fac'd children, and as lovely,   35
As you'll be Mother of; I will not spare you:
What cannot children be begot think you,
Without gilt casting Bottles? Yes, and as sweet ones.
The Millers daughter brings forth as white boys,
As she that bathes her self with Milk and Bean flower.   40
'Tis an old saying, One may keep good cheer
In a mean house; so may true love affect
After the rate of Princes in a Cottage.
BRANCHA.   Troth you speak wondrous well for your old house
here;
'Twill shortly fall down at your feet to thank you,   45
Or stoop when you go to Bed, like a good childe
To ask you blessing. Must I live in want,
Because my fortune matcht me with your Son?

Wives do not give away themselves to husbands,
To the end to be quite cast away; they look   50
To be the better us'd, and tender'd rather,
Highlier respected, and maintain'd the richer;
They're well rewarded else for the free gift
Of their whole life to a husband. I ask less now
Then what I had at home when I was a Maid,   55
And at my Fathers house, kept short of that
Which a wife knows she must have, nay, and will;
Will Mother, if she be not a fool born;
And report went of me, that I could wrangle
For what I wanted when I was two hours old,   60
And by that copy, this Land still I hold.
You hear me Mother.

                                                    Exit.

MOTHER.   I too plain methinks;
And were I somewhat deafer when you spake,
'Twere nev'r a whit the worse for my quietness.   65
'Tis the most sudden'st, strangest alteration,
And the most subtilest that ev'r wit at threescore
Was puzzled to finde out: I know no cause for't; but
She's no more like the Gentlewoman at first,
Then I am like her that nev'r lay with man yet,   70
And she's a very yong thing where ere she be;
When she first lighted here, I told her then
How mean she should finde all things; she was pleas'd
forsooth,
None better: I laid open all defects to her,
She was contented still; but the Devil's in her,   75
Nothing contents her now: To night my Son
Promisd to be at home, would he were come once,
For I'm weary of my charge, and life too:
She'ld be serv'd all in silver by her good will,
By night and day; she hates the name of Pewterer,   80
More then sick men the noise, or diseas'd bones
That quake at fall o'th' Hammer, seeming to have
A fellow-feeling with't at every blow:
What course shall I think on? she frets me so.

                                                    ⟨*Exit.*⟩

Enter LEANTIO.

LEANTIO. How near am I now to a happiness,   85
 That Earth exceeds not? not another like it;
 The treasures of the deep are not so precious,
 As are the conceal'd comforts of a man,
 Lockt up in womans love. I sent the air
 Of Blessings when I come but near the house;   90
 What a delicious breath Marriage sends forth!
 The Violet-beds not sweeter. Honest wedlock
 Is like a Banquetting-house built in a Garden,
 On which the Springs chaste flowers take delight
 To cast their modest odors; when base Lust   95
 With all her powders, paintings, and best pride,
 Is but a fair house built by a Ditch side.
 When I behold a glorious dangerous Strumpet,
 Sparkling in Beauty and Destruction too,
 Both at a twinkling, I do liken straight   100
 Her beautifi'd body to a goodly Temple
 That's built on Vaults where Carkasses lie rotting,
 And so by little and little I shrink back again,
 And quench desire with a cool Meditation,
 And I'm as well methinks: Now for a welcome   105
 Able to draw mens envies upon man:
 A kiss now that will hang upon my lip,
 As sweet as morning dew upon a Rose,
 And full as long; after a five days fast
 She'll be so greedy now, and cling about me;   110
 I take care how I shall be rid of her,
 And here't begins.

⟨*Enter* BRANCHA *and* MOTHER.⟩

BRANCHA. Oh Sir, y'are welcome home.
MOTHER. Oh is he come, I am glad on't.
LEANTIO. Is that all?   115
 Why this? as dreadful now as sudden death
 To some rich man, that flatters all his sins
 With promise of Repentance, when he's old,
 And dies in the midway before he comes to't.
 Sure, y'are not well, *Brancha*! How do'st prethee?   120

BRANCHA.   I have been better then I am at this time.

LEANTIO.   Alas, I thought so.

BRANCHA.   Nay, I have been worse too,
  Then now you see me Sir.

LEANTIO.   I'm glad thou mendst yet,   125
  I feel my heart mend too: How came it to thee?
  Has any thing dislik'd thee in my absence?

BRANCHA.   No certain, I have had the best content
  That *Florence* can afford.

LEANTIO.   Thou makest the best on't,   130
  Speak Mother, what's the cause? you must needs know.

MOTHER.   Troth I know none Son, let her speak her self;
  Unless it be the same gave *Lucifer* a tumbling cast; that's pride.

BRANCHA.   Methinks this house stands nothing to my minde;
  I'ld have some pleasant lodging i'th' high street Sir,   135
  Or if 'twere neer the Court Sir, that were much better;
  'Tis a sweet recreation for a Gentlewoman,
  To stand in a Bay-window, and see gallants.

LEANTIO.   Now I have another temper, a meer stranger
  To that of yours, it seems; I should delight   140
  To see none but your self.

BRANCHA.   I praise not that:
  Too fond is as unseemly as too churlish;
  I would not have a husband of that proneness,
  To kiss me before company, for a world: 145
  Beside 'tis tedious to see one thing still (Sir)
  Be it the best that ever heart affected;
  Nay, wer't your self, whose love had power you know
  To bring me from my friends, I would not stand thus,
  And gaze upon you always: Troth I could not Sir;   150
  As good be blinde, and have no use of sight
  As look on one thing still: What's the eyes treasure,
  But change of objects? You are learned Sir,
  And know I speak not ill; 'tis full as vertuous
  For womans eye to look on several men,   155
  As for her heart (Sir) to be fixed on one.

LEANTIO.   Now thou com'st home to me; a kiss for that word.

BRANCHA.   No matter for a kiss Sir, let it pass,
  'Tis but a toy, we'll not so much as minde it,

Let's talk of other business, and forget it.   160
What news now of the Pirats, any stirring?
Prethee discourse a little.
MOTHER. ⟨*Aside.*⟩   I am glad he's here yet
  To see her tricks himself; I had lied monst'rously,
  If I had told 'em first.   165
LEANTIO.   Speak what's the humor (Sweet)
  You make your lip so strange? this was not wont.
BRANCHA.   Is there no kindness betwixt man and wife,
  Unless they make a Pigeon-house of friendship,
  And be still billing; 'tis the idlest fondness   170
  That ever was invented, and 'tis pity
  Its grown a fashion for poor Gentlewomen;
  There's many a disease kiss'd in a year by't,
  And a French cursie made to't: Alas Sir,
  Think of the world, how we shall live, grow serious,   175
  We have been married a whole fortnight now.
LEANTIO.   How? a whole fortnight! why is that so long?
BRANCHA.   'Tis time to leave off dalliance; 'tis a doctrine
  Of your own teaching, if you be remembred,
  And I was bound to obey it.   180
MOTHER.   Here's one fits him;
  This was well catch'd y'faith Son, like a fellow
  That rids another Countrey of a Plague,
  And brings it home with him to his own house.
                                        Knock within.

Who knocks?   185
LEANTIO.   Who's there now? withdraw you *Brancha*,
  Thou art a Jem no strangers eye must see,
  How ev'r thou please now to look dull on me.
                                        Exit ⟨BRANCHA⟩.
Enter MESSENGER.

Y'are welcome Sir; to whom your business, pray?
MESSENGER.   To one I see not here now.   190
LEANTIO.   Who should that be Sir?
MESSENGER.   A yong Gentlewoman, I was sent to.
LEANTIO.   A yong Gentlewoman?
              188 please] SIMPSON; pleas'd TNP.

MESSENGER.   I Sir, about sixteen; why look you wildly Sir?

LEANTIO.   At your strange error: Y'have mistook the house Sir.   195
  There's none such here, I assure you.

MESSENGER.   I assure you too,
  The man that sent me, cannot be mistook.

LEANTIO.   Why, who is't sent you Sir?

MESSENGER.   The Duke.   200

LEANTIO.   The Duke?

MESSENGER.   Yes, he entreates her company at a Banquet
  At Lady *Livia*'s house.

LEANTIO.   Troth shall I tell you Sir,
  It is the most erroneous business   205
  That ere your honest pains was abus'd with;
  I pray forgive me, if I smile a little,
  I cannot chuse y'faith Sir, at an error
  So Comical as this (I mean no harm though)
  His grace has been most wondrous ill inform'd,   210
  Pray so return it (Sir). What should her name be?

MESSENGER.   That I shall tell you straight too, *Brancha Capella*.

LEANTIO.   How Sir, *Brancha*? What do you call th'other.

MESSENGER.   *Capella*; Sir, it seems you know no such then?

LEANTIO.   Who should this be? I never heard o'th' name.   215

MESSENGER.   Then 'tis a sure mistake.

LEANTIO.   What if you enquir'd
  In the next street Sir? I saw Gallants there
  In the new houses that are built of late.
  Ten to one, there you finde her.   220

MESSENGER.   Nay no matter,
  I will return the mistake, and seek no further.

LEANTIO.   Use your own will and pleasure Sir, y'are welcome.

Exit MESSENGER.

What shall I think of first? Come forth *Brancha*,
Thou art betraid I fear me.   225

Enter BRANCHA.

BRANCHA.   Betraid, how Sir?

LEANTIO.   The Duke knows thee.

BRANCHA.   Knows me! how know you that Sir?

W.B.W.—3*

LEANTIO.   Has got thy name.

BRANCHA. ⟨*Aside.*⟩   I, and my good name too,   230
That's worse o'th' twain.

LEANTIO.   How comes this work about?

BRANCHA.   How should the Duke know me? can you ghess
Mother?

MOTHER.   Not I with all my wits, sure we kept house close.

LEANTIO.   Kept close! not all the Locks in *Italy*   235
Can keep you women so; you have been gadding,
And ventur'd out at twilight, to th' Court-green yonder,
And met the gallant Bowlers coming home;
Without your Masks too, both of you, I'll be hang'd else;
Thou hast been seen *Brancha* by some stranger;   240
Never excuse it.

BRANCHA.   I'll not seek the way Sir;
Do you think y'have married me to mew me up
Not to be seen; what would you make of me?

LEANTIO.   A good wife, nothing else.   245

BRANCHA.   Why, so are some
That are seen ev'ry day, else the Devil take 'em.

LEANTIO.   No more then I believe all vertuous in thee,
Without an argument; 'twas but thy hard chance
To be seen somewhere, there lies all the mischief;   250
But I have devis'd a riddance.

MOTHER.   Now I can tell you Son,
The time and place.

LEANTIO.   When, where?

MOTHER.   What wits have I?   255
When you last took your leave, if you remember,
You left us both at Window.

LEANTIO.   Right, I know that.

MOTHER.   And not the third part of an hour after,
The Duke past by in a great solemnity,   260
To St. *Marks* Temple, and to my apprehension
He look'd up twice to th' Window.

LEANTIO.   Oh there quick'ned
The mischeif of this hour!

BRANCHA. ⟨*Aside.*⟩   If you call't mischeif,   265
It is a thing I fear I am conceiv'd with.

LEANTIO.   Look'd he up twice, and could you take no warning!
MOTHER.   Why once may do as much harm Son, as a thousand;
  Do not you know one spark has fir'd an house,
  As well as a whole Furnace?   270
LEANTIO.   My heart flames for't,
  Yet let's be wise, and keep all smother'd closely;
  I have bethought a means; is the door fast?
MOTHER.   I lockt it my self after him.
LEANTIO.   You know Mother,   275
  At the end of the dark Parlor there's a place
  So artificially contriv'd for a Conveyance,
  No search could ever finde it: When my Father
  Kept in for man-slaughter, it was his Sanctuary;
  There will I lock my lifes best treasure up.   280
  Brancha?
BRANCHA.   Would you keep me closer yet?
  Have you the conscience? y'are best ev'n choke me up Sir?
  You make me fearful of your health and wits,
  You cleave to such wilde courses, what's the matter?   285
LEANTIO.   Why, are you so insensible of your danger
  To ask that now? the Duke himself has sent for you
  To Lady *Livia*'s, to a Banquet forsooth.
BRANCHA.   Now I beshrew you heartily, has he so!
  And you the man would never yet vouchsafe   290
  To tell me on't till now: You shew your loyalty
  And honesty at once, and so farewel Sir.
LEANTIO.   *Brancha*, whether now?
BRANCHA.   Why to the Duke Sir.
  You say he sent for me.   295
LEANTIO.   But thou dost not mean to go, I hope.
BRANCHA.   No? I shall prove unmannerly,
  Rude, and uncivil, mad, and imitate you.
  Come Mother come, follow his humor no longer,
  We shall be all executed for treason shortly.   300
MOTHER.   Not I y'faith; I'll first obey the Duke,
  And taste of a good Banquet, I'm of thy minde.
  I'll step but up, and fetch two Handkerchiefs
  To pocket up some Sweet-meats, and o'r take thee.
                                                         Exit.

BRANCHA. ⟨*Aside.*⟩   Why here's an old Wench would trot into a
    Baud now,   305
    For some dry Sucket, or a Colt in March-pain.

                                                                 Exit.

LEANTIO.   Oh thou the ripe time of mans misery, wedlock;
    When all his thoughts like over laden Trees,
    Crack with the Fruits they bear, in cares, in jealousies.
    Oh that's a fruit that ripens hastily,   310
    After 'tis knit to marriage; it begins
    As soon as the Sun shines upon the Bride
    A little to shew colour. Blessed Powers!
    Whence comes this alteration! the distractions,
    The fears and doubts it brings are numberless,   315
    And yet the cause I know not: What a peace
    Has he that never marries! if he knew
    The benefit he enjoy'd, or had the fortune
    To come and speak with me, he should know then
    The infinite wealth he had, and discern rightly   320
    The greatness of his treasure by my loss:
    Nay, what a quietness has he 'bove mine,
    That wears his youth out in a strumpets arms,
    And never spends more care upon a woman,
    Then at the time of Lust; but walks away,   325
    And if he finde her dead at his return,
    His pitty is soon done, he breaks a sigh
    In many parts, and gives her but a peece on't!
    But all the fears, shames, jealousies, costs and troubles,
    And still renew'd cares of a marriage Bed,   330
    Live in the issue, when the wife is dead.

Enter MESSENGER.

MESSENGER.   A good perfection to your thoughts.
LEANTIO.   The news Sir?
MESSENGER.   Though you were pleas'd of late to pin an error
    on me,
    You must not shift another in your stead too: 335
    The Duke has sent me for you.
LEANTIO.   How for me Sir?

⟨*Aside.*⟩ I see then 'tis my theft; w'are both betraid.
Well, I'm not the first h'as stoln away a Maid,
My Countrymen have us'd it: I'll along with you Sir.   340

Exeunt.

SCENE II

A Banquet prepared: Enter GUARDIANO *and* WARD.

GUARDIANO.   Take you especial note of such a Gentlewoman,
    She's here on purpose, I have invited her,
    Her Father, and her Uncle, to this Banquet;
    Mark her behavior well, it does concern you;
    And what her good parts are, as far as time   5
    And place can modestly require a knowledge of,
    Shall be laid open to your understanding.
    You know I'm both your Guardian, and your Uncle,
    My care of you is double, Ward and Nephew,
    And I'll express it here.   10
WARD.   Faith, I should know her
    Now by her mark among a thousand women:
    A lettle pretty deft and tidy thing you say.
GUARDIANO.   Right.
WARD.   With a lusty sprouting sprig in her hair.   15
GUARDIANO.   Thou goest the right way still; take one mark
        more,
    Thou shalt nev'r finde her hand out of her Uncles,
    Or else his out of hers, if she be near him:
    The love of kinred, never yet stuck closer
    Then their's to one another; he that weds her,   20
    Marries her Uncles heart too.

Cornets.

WARD.   Say you so Sir,
    Then I'll be ask'd i'th' Church to both of them.
GUARDIANO.   Fall back, here comes the Duke.
WARD.   He brings a Gentlewoman,   25
    I should fall forward rather.

Enter DUKE, BRANCHA, FABRITIO, HIPPOLITO, LIVIA,

MOTHER, ISABELLA, *and Attendants.*

DUKE.   Come *Brancha,*
    Of purpose sent into the world to shew
    Perfection once in woman; I'll believe
    Hence forward they have ev'ry one a Soul too   30
    'Gainst all the uncurteous opinions
    That mans uncivil rudeness ever held of 'em:
    Glory of *Florence* light into mine arms!

Enter LEANTIO.

BRANCHA.   Yon comes a grudging man will chide you Sir;
    The storm is now in's heart, and would get nearer,   35
    And fall here if it durst, it powres done yonder.
DUKE.   If that be he, the weather shall soon clear.
    List, and I'll tell thee how.

                                ⟨*Whispers to her.*⟩

LEANTIO. ⟨*Aside.*⟩   A kissing too?
    I see 'tis plain Lust now; Adultery boldned;   40
    What will it prove anon, when 'tis stufft full
    Of Wine and Sweet-meats, being so impudent Fasting?
DUKE.   We have heard of your good parts Sir, which we honor
    With our embrace and love; is not the Captainship
    Of *Rouans* Cittadel, since the late deceas'd,   45
    Suppli'd by any yet?
GENTLEMAN.   By none my Lord.
DUKE.   Take it, the place is yours then, and as faithfulness
    And desert grows, our favor shall grow with't:
    Rise now the Captain of our Fort at *Rouans.*   50
LEANTIO.   The service of whole life give your Grace thanks.
DUKE.   Come sit *Brancha.*
LEANTIO. ⟨*Aside.*⟩   This is some good yet,
    And more then ev'r I look'd for, a fine bit
    To stay a Cuckolds stomach: All preferment   55
    That springs from sin and lust, it shoots up quickly,
    As Gardiners crops do in the rotten'st grounds;
    So is all means rais'd from base prostitution,
    Ev'n like a Sallet growing upon a dunghil:
    I'm like a thing that never was yet heard of,   60
    Half merry, and half mad, much like a fellow

That eats his meat with a good appetite,
And wears a plague-sore that would fright a Country;
Or rather like the barren hardned Ass,
That feeds on Thistles till he bleeds again;   65
And such is the condition of my misery.
LIVIA.   Is that your Son widow?
MOTHER.   Yes, did your Ladiship never know that till now?
LIVIA.   No trust me did I,
⟨*Aside.*⟩ Nor ever truly felt the power of love,   70
And pitty to a man, till now I knew him;
I have enough to buy me my desires,
And yet to spare; that's one good comfort. Hark you?
⟨*To* LEANTIO.⟩ Pray let me speak with you Sir, before you go.
LEANTIO.   With me Lady? you shall, I am at your service: 75
⟨*Aside.*⟩ What will she say now trow, more goodness yet?
WARD.   I see her now I'm sure; the Ape's so little,
I shall scarce feel her; I have seen almost
As tall as she, sold in the Fair for ten pence.
See how she simpers it, as if Marmalad   80
Would not melt in her mouth; she might have the kindness
y'faith
To send me a guilded Bull from her own Trencher,
A Ram, a Goat, or somewhat to be nibling.
These women when they come to sweet things once,
They forget all their friends, they grow so greedy;   85
Nay, oftentimes their husbands.
DUKE.   Here's a health now Gallants,
To the best beauty at this day in *Florence*.
BRANCHA.   Who ere she be, she shall not go unpledg'd Sir.
DUKE.   Nay, your excus'd for this.   90
BRANCHA.   Who I my Lord?
DUKE.   Yes by the Law of *Bacchus*; plead your benefit,
You are not bound to pledge your own health Lady.
BRANCHA.   That's a good way my Lord to keep me dry.
DUKE.   Nay, then I will not offend *Venus* so much,   95
Let *Bacchus* seek his mends in another Court,
Here's to thy self *Brancha*.
BRANCHA.   Nothing comes
More welcome to that name then your Grace.

LEANTIO. ⟨*Aside.*⟩ So, so;   100
   Here stands the poor theif now that stole the treasure,
   And he's not thought on, ours is near kin now
   To a twin-misery born into the world.
   First the hard-conscienc'd worldling, he hoords wealth up,
   Then comes the next, and he feasts all upon't;   105
   One's damn'd for getting, th'other for spending on't.
   Oh equal Justice, thou has't met my sin
   With a full weight, I'm rightly now opprest,
   All her friends heavy hearts lie in my Brest.

DUKE.   Methinks there is no spirit amongst us Gallants,   110
   But what divinely sparkles from the eyes
   Of bright *Brancha*; we sat all in darkness,
   But for that Splendor: Who was't told us lately
   Of a match making right, a marriage tender?

GUARDIANO.   'Twas I my Lord.   115

DUKE.   'Twas you indeed: Where is she?

GUARDIANO.   This is the Gentlewoman.

FABRITIO.   My Lord, my Daughter.

DUKE.   Why here's some stirring yet.

FABRITIO.   She's a dear childe to me.   120

DUKE.   That must needs be; you say she is your Daughter.

FABRITIO.   Nay, my good Lord, dear to my purse I mean
   Beside my person, I nev'r reckon'd that.
   She has the full qualities of a Gentlewoman;
   I have brought her up to Musick, Dancing, what not,   125
   That may commend her Sex, and stir her husband?

DUKE.   And which is he now?

GUARDIANO.   This yong Heir, my Lord.

DUKE.   What is he brought up too?

HIPPOLITO. ⟨*Aside.*⟩   To Cat and Trap.   130

GUARDIANO.   My Lord, he's a great Ward, wealthy, but simple;
   His parts consist in Acres.

DUKE.   Oh Wise-acres.

GUARDIANO.   Y'have spoke him in a word Sir.

BRANCHA.   'Lass poor Gentlewoman,   135
   She's ill bestead, unless sh'as dealt the wiselier,
   And laid in more provision for her youth:
   Fools will not keep in Summer.

LEANTIO. ⟨*Aside.*⟩   No, nor such wives
  From whores in winter.   140
DUKE.   Yea, the voice too Sir!
FABRITIO.   I, and a sweet Brest too my Lord, I hope,
  Or I have cast away my money wisely;
  She took her pricksong earlier, my Lord,
  Then any of her kinred ever did: 145
  A rare childe, though I say't, but I'ld not have
  The Baggage hear so much, 'twould make her swell straight:
  And Maids of all things must not be puft up.
DUKE.   Let's turn us to a better Banquet then,
  For Musick bids the soul of a man to a Feast,   150
  And that's indeed, a noble entertainment,
  Worthy *Brancha*'s self; you shall perceive Beauty,
  Our *Florentine* Damsels are not brought up idlely.
BRANCHA.   They'are wiser of themselves, it seems my Lord,
  And can take gifts, when goodness offers 'em.   155

                                        Musick.

LEANTIO. ⟨*Aside.*⟩   True, and damnation has taught you that
  wisdom,
  You can take gifts too. Oh that Musick mocks me!
LIVIA. ⟨*Aside.*⟩   I am as dumb to any language now
  But Loves, as one that never learn'd to speak:
  I am not yet so old, but he may think of me;   160
  My own fault, I have been idle a long time;
  But I'll begin the week, and paint to morrow,
  So follow my true labor day by day.
  I never thriv'd so well, as when I us'd it.
⟨ISABELLA *sings.*⟩

SONG

      W*Hat harder chance can fall to woman,*   165
      Who was born to cleave to some-man,
      Then to bestow her time, youth, beauty,
      Life's observance, honor, duty,
      On a thing for no use good,
      But to make Physick work, or blood force fresh   170
      In an old Ladies cheek, she that would be
      Mother of fools, let her compound with me.

WARD.   Here's a tune indeed; Pish I had rather hear one Ballad
  sung i'th' Nose now, of the lamentable drowning of fat Sheep and
  Oxen, then all these simpering tunes plaid upon Cats-guts, and   175
  sung by little Kitlings.
FABRITIO.   How like you her Brest now my Lord?
BRANCHA.   Her Brest?
  He talks as if his daughter had given suck
  Before she were married, as her betters have;   18c
  The next he praises sure, will be her Nipples.
DUKE.   Methinks now, such a voice to such a husband,
  Is like a Jewel of unvalued worth,
  Hung at a Fools ear.
FABRITIO.   May it please your Grace   185
  To give her leave to shew another Quality.
DUKE.   Marry as many good ones as you will Sir,
  The more the better welcome.
LEANTIO. ⟨Aside.⟩   But the less
  The better practis'd: That soul's black indeed   190
  That cannot commend Vertue; but who keeps it!
  The Extortioner will say to a sick begger,
  Heaven comfort thee, though he give none himself:
  This good is common.
FABRITIO.   Will it please you now Sir,   195
  To entreat your Ward to take her by the hand,
  And lead her in a dance before the Duke?
GUARDIANO.   That will I Sir, 'tis needful; hark you Nephew.

                              ⟨Speaks aside to the WARD.⟩

FABRITIO.   Nay, you shall see yong heir, what y'have for your
  money,
  Without fraud or imposture.   200
WARD.   Dance with her!
  Not I sweet Gardiner, do not urge my heart to't,
  'Tis clean against my Blood; dance with a stranger!
  Let who's will do't, I'll not begin first with her.
HIPPOLITO. ⟨Aside.⟩   No fear't not fool, sh'as took a better
  order.   205
GUARDIANO.   Why who shall take her then?
WARD.   Some other Gentleman;

Look, there's her Uncle, a fine timber'd Reveller,
Perhaps he knows the manner of her dancing too,
I'll have him do't before me, I have sworn Gardiner,   210
Then may I learn the better.
GUARDIANO.   Thou'lt be an ass still.
WARD.   I, all that Uncle, shall not fool me out.
Pish, I stick closer to my self then so.
GUARDIANO.   I must entreat you Sir, to take your Neece   215
And dance with her; my Ward's a little wilful,
He would have you shew him the way.
HIPPOLITO.   Me Sir?
He shall command it at all hours, pray tell him so.
GUARDIANO.   I thank you for him, he has not wit himself Sir.   220
HIPPOLITO. ⟨*Aside to* ISABELLA.⟩   Come my life's peace, I have
a strange office on't here,
'Tis some mans luck to keep the joys he likes
Conceal'd for his own bosom; but my fortune
To set 'em out now, for anothers liking,
Like the mad misery of necessitous man,   225
That parts from his good horse with many praises,
And goes on foot himself; need must be obey'd
In ev'ry action, it mars man and maid.

                                                      Musick.

A dance, making Honors to the DUKE *and cursie to themselves,*
both before and after.

DUKE.   Signior *Fabritio*, y'are a happy Father,
Your cares and pains are fortunate you see,   230
Your cost bears noble fruits. *Hippolito* thanks.
FABRITIO.   Here's some amends for all my charges yet.
She wins both prick and praise, where ere she comes.
DUKE.   How lik'st *Brancha?*
BRANCHA.   All things well, my Lord: 235
But this poor Gentlewomans fortune, that's the worst.
DUKE.   There is no doubt *Brancha*, she'll finde leisure
To make that good enough; he's rich and simple.
BRANCHA.   She has the better hope o'th' upper hand indeed,
Which women strive for most.   240
GUARDIANO.   Do't when I bid you Sir.

WARD.   I'll venture but a Horn-pipe with her Gardiner,
   Or some such married mans dance.
GUARDIANO.   Well venture something Sir.
WARD.   I have rime for what I do.   245
GUARDIANO.   But little reason, I think.
WARD.   Plain men dance the Measures, the Sinquapace, the Gay:
   Cuckolds dance the Horn-pipe; and Farmers dance the Hay:
   Your Soldiers dance the Round, and Maidens that grow big:
   Your Drunkards, the Canaries; your Whore and Baud, the Jigg. 250
   Here's your eight kinde of Dancers, he that findes the nineth, let him
   Pay the Minstrels.
DUKE.   Oh here he appears once in his own person;
   I thought he would have married her by Attorney,
   And lain with her so too.   255
BRANCHA.   Nay, my kinde Lord,
   There's very seldom any found so foolish
   To give away his part there.
LEANTIO. ⟨*Aside.*⟩   Bitter scoff;
   Yet I must do't; with what a cruel pride   *Musick.*   260
   The glory of her sin strikes by my afflictions.

WARD *and* ISABELLA *dance, he ridiculously imitates* HIPPOLITO.

DUKE.   This thing will make shift (Sirs) to make a husband,
   For ought I see in him; how thinks't *Brancha*?
BRANCHA.   'Faith an ill-favored shift my Lord, methinks;
   If he would take some voyage when he's married,   265
   Dangerous, or long enough, and scarce be seen
   Once in nine year together, a wife then
   Might make indifferent shift to be content with him.
DUKE.   A kiss; that wit deserves to be made much on:
   Come, our Caroch.   270
GUARDIANO.   Stands ready for your Grace.
DUKE.   My thanks to all your loves: Come fair *Brancha*,
   We have took special care of you, and provided
   Your lodging near us now.

III. II. 244 Well] DILKE; We'll TNP.
   250 Your] DILKE; You TNP.
   250 your] DILKE; you TNP.
   260 pride‿] DILKE; pride! TNP.

BRANCHA.   Your love is great, my Lord.   275
DUKE.   Once more our thanks to all.
OMNES.   All blest Honors guard you.

Exeunt all but LEANTIO *and* LIVIA; *Cornets flourish.*

LEANTIO.   Oh hast thou left me then *Brancha*, utterly!
    Brancha! now I miss thee; Oh return!
    And save the faith of woman; I nev'r felt   280
    The loss of thee till now; 'tis an affliction
    Of greater weight, then youth was made to bear;
    As if a punishment of after-life
    Were faln upon man here; so new it is
    To flesh and blood, so strange, so insupportable   285
    A torment, ev'n mistooke, as if a body
    Whose death were drowning, must needs therefore suffer it in
    scalding oyl.
LIVIA.   Sweet Sir!
LEANTIO.   As long as mine eye saw thee,
    I half enjoy'd thee.   290
LIVIA.   Sir?
LEANTIO.   Canst thou forget
    The dear pains my love took, how it has watch't
    Whole nights together, in all weathers for thee,
    Yet stood in heart more merry then the tempests   295
    That sung about mine ears, like dangerous flatterers
    That can set all their mischeif to sweet tunes;
    And then receiv'd thee from thy fathers window,
    Into these arms at midnight, when we embrac'd
    As if we had been Statues onely made for't,   300
    To shew arts life, so silent were our comforts,
    And kiss'd as if our lips had grown together!
LIVIA.   This makes me madder to enjoy him now.
LEANTIO.   Canst thou forget all this? And better joys
    That we met after this, which then new kisses   305
    Took pride to praise.
LIVIA.   I shall grow madder yet, Sir—
LEANTIO.   This cannot be but of some close Bauds working:
    Cry mercy Lady. What would you say to me?

My sorrow makes me so unmannerly,   310
So comfort bless me, I had quite forgot you.
LIVIA.   Nothing but ev'n in pitty to that passion
Would give your grief good counsel.
LEANTIO.   Marry, and welcome Lady,
It never could come better.   315
LIVIA.   Then first Sir,
To make away all your good thoughts at once of her,
Know most assuredly, she is a strumpet.
LEANTIO.   Ha: Most assuredly! Speak not a thing
So vilde so certainly, leave it more doubtful.   320
LIVIA.   Then I must leave all truth, and spare my knowledge,
A sin which I too lately found and wept for.
LEANTIO.   Found you it?
LIVIA.   I with wet eyes.
LEANTIO.   Oh perjurious friendship!   325
LIVIA.   You miss'd your fortunes when you met with her Sir.
Yong Gentlemen, that onely love for beauty,
They love not wisely; such a marriage rather
Proves the destruction of affection;
It brings on want, and want's the Key of whoredom.   330
I think y'had small means with her.
LEANTIO.   Oh not any Lady.
LIVIA.   Alas poor Gentleman, what meant'st thou Sir,
Quite to undo thy self with thine own kinde heart?
Thou art too good and pitiful to woman: 335
Marry Sir, thank thy Stars for this blest fortune
That rids the Summer of thy youth so well
From many Beggers that had lain a sunning
In thy beams onely else, till thou hadst wasted
The whole days of thy life in heat and labor.   340
What would you say now to a Creature found
As pitiful to you, and as it were
Ev'n sent on purpose from the whole Sex general,
To requite all that kindness you have shewn to't?
LEANTIO.   What's that Madam?   345
LIVIA.   Nay, a Gentlewoman, and one able
To reward good things, I, and bears a conscience to't;

Couldst thou love such a one, that (blow all fortunes)
Would never see thee want?
Nay more, maintain thee to thine enemies envy,   350
And shalt not spend a care for't, stir a thought,
Nor break a sleep, unless loves musick waked thee;
No storm of fortune should; look upon me,
And know that woman.
LEANTIO.   Oh my life's wealth *Brancha*!   355
LIVIA.   Still with her name? will nothing wear it out?
That deep sigh went but for a strumpet Sir.
LEANTIO.   It can go for no other that loves me.
LIVIA. ⟨*Aside.*⟩   He's vext in minde; I came too soon to him;
Where's my discretion now, my skill, my judgment?   360
I'm cunning in all arts but my own, love:
'Tis as unseasonable to tempt him now
So soon, as a widow to be courted
Following her husbands coarse, or to make bargain
By the grave side, and take a yong man there: 365
Her strange departure stands like a herse yet
Before his eyes; which time will take down shortly.

                                                    Exit.

LEANTIO.   Is she my wife till death? yet no more mine;
That's a hard measure; then what's marriage good for?
Me thinks by right, I should not now be living,   370
And then 'twere all well: What a happiness
Had I been made of, had I never seen her;
For nothing makes mans loss grievous to him,
But knowledge of the worth of what he loses;
For what he never had, he never misses: 375
She's gone for ever, utterly; there is
As much redemption of a soul from Hell,
As a fair womans body from his pallace.
Why should my love last longer then her truth?
What is there good in woman to be lov'd,   380
When onely that which makes her so, has left her?
I cannot love her now, but I must like

353 should;] ∼ₐ TNP.   376 ever, utterly;] DILKE; ∼; utterly ₐ TNP.

Her sin, and my own shame too, and be guilty
Of Laws breach with her, and mine own abusing;
All which were monstrous: Then my safest course   385
For health of minde and body, is to turn
My heart, and hate her, most extreamly hate her;
I have no other way: Those vertuous powers
Which were chaste witnesses of both our troths,
Can witness she breaks first, and I'm rewarded   390
With Captainship o'th' Fort; a place of credit
I must confess, but poor; my Factorship
Shall not exchange means with't: He that di'd last in't,
He was no drunkard, yet he di'd a begger
For all his thrift; besides the place not fits me;   395
It suits my resolution, not my breeding.

Enter LIVIA.

LIVIA. ⟨*Aside.*⟩   I have tri'd all ways I can, and have not power
    To keep from sight of him: How are you now Sir?
LEANTIO.   I feel a better ease Madam.
LIVIA.   Thanks to blessedness.   400
    You will do well I warrant you, fear it not Sir;
    Joyn but your own good will to't; he's not wise
    That loves his pain or sickness, or grows fond
    Of a disease, whose property is to vex him,
    And spightfully drink his blood up: Out upon't Sir,   405
    Youth knows no greater loss; I pray let's walk Sir.
    You never saw the beauty of my house yet,
    Nor how abundantly Fortune has blest me
    In worldly treasure; trust me I have enough Sir
    To make my friend a rich man in my life,   410
    A great man at my death; your self will say so.
    If you want any thing, and spare to speak,
    Troth I'll condemn you for a wilful man Sir.
LEANTIO.   Why sure this can be but the flattery of some dream.
LIVIA.   Now by this kiss, my love, my soul and riches,   415
    'Tis all true substance.
    Come you shall see my wealth, take what you list,
    The gallanter you go, the more you please me:
    I will allow you too, your Page and Footman,

Your race horses, or any various pleasure   420
Exercis'd youth delights in; but to me
Onely Sir wear your heart of constant stuff:
Do but you love enough, I'll give enough.
LEANTIO.   Troth then, I'll love enough, and take enough.
LIVIA.   Then we are both pleas'd enough.   425

Exeunt.

SCENE III

Enter GUARDIANO *and* ISABELLA *at one door, and the*
WARD *and* SORDIDO *at another.*

GUARDIANO.   Now Nephew, here's the Gentlewoman again.
WARD.   Mass here she's come again; mark her now *Sordido.*
GUARDIANO.   This is the Maid, my love and care has chose
   Out for your wife, and so I tender her to you;
   Your self has been eye witness of some qualities   5
   That speak a courtly breeding, and are costly.
   I bring you both to talk together now,
   'Tis time you grew familiar in your tongues;
   To morrow you joyn hands, and one Ring ties you,
   And one Bed holds you (if you like the choice),   10
   Her Father and her friends are i'th' next room,
   And stay to see the contract ere they part;
   Therefore dispatch good Ward, be sweet and short;
   Like her, or like her not, there's but two ways;
   And one your body, th'other your purse pays.   15
WARD.   I warrant you Gardiner, I'll not stand all day thruming,
   But quickly shoot my bolt at your next coming.
GUARDIANO.   Well said: Good fortune to your birding then.

⟨*Exit.*⟩

WARD.   I never miss'd mark yet.
SORDIDO.   Troth I think Master, if the truth were known,   20
   You never shot at any but the Kitchin-wench,
   And that was a she-woodcock, a meer innocent,
   That was oft lost, and cri'd at eight and twenty.

WARD.   No more of that meat *Sordido*, here's Eggs o'th' spit now,
We must turn gingerly, draw out the Catalogue   25
Of all the faults of women.

SORDIDO.   How, all the faults! have you so little reason to
think so much Paper will lie in my breeches? why ten carts will
not carry it, if you set down but the Bauds; all the faults? pray
let's be content with a few of 'em; and if they were less, you   30
would finde 'em enough I warrant you: Look you Sir.

⟨*Takes out a paper.*⟩

ISABELLA. ⟨*Aside.*⟩   But that I have th'advantage of the fool,
As much as womans heart can wish and joy at,
What an infernal torment 'twere to be
Thus bought and sold, and turn'd and pri'd into; when alass   35
The worst bit is too good for him? and the comfort is
H'as but a Caters place on't, and provides
All for anothers table; yet how curious
The Ass is, like some nice professor on't,
That buys up all the daintiest food i'th' Markets,   40
And seldom licks his lips after a taste on't!

SORDIDO.   Now to her, now y'have scand all her parts over.

WARD.   But at which end shall I begin now *Sordido*?

SORDIDO.   Oh ever at a womans lip, while you live Sir, do you
ask that question?   45

WARD.   Methinks *Sordido*, sh'as but a crabbed face to begin with.

SORDIDO.   A crabbed face? that will save money.

WARD.   How! save money *Sordido*?

SORDIDO.   I Sir: For having a crabbed face of her own, she'll
eat the less Verjuyce with her Mutton; 'twill save Verjuyce at   50
years end Sir.

WARD.   Nay and your jests begin to be sawcy once, I'll make you
eat your meat without Mustard.

SORDIDO.   And that in some kinde is a punishment.

WARD.   Gentlewoman, they say 'tis your pleasure to be my   55
wife, and you shall know shortly whether it be mine or no, to
be your husband; and thereupon thus I first enter upon you.

⟨*Kisses her.*⟩

Oh most delicious scent! Methinks it tasted as if a man had

III. III. 43 at which] DILKE; at TNP.

stept into a Comfit-makers shop to let a Cart go by, all the
while I kiss'd her: It is reported Gentlewoman you'll run mad   60
    for me, if you have me not.

ISABELLA.   I should be in great danger of my wits Sir,
    ⟨*Aside.*⟩   For being so forward, should this Ass kick backward
    now.

WARD.   Alass poor Soul! And is that hair your own?

ISABELLA.   Mine own, yes sure Sir, I ow nothing for't.   65

WARD.   'Tis a good hearing, I shall have the less to pay when I
    have married you: Look, does her eyes stand well?

SORDIDO.   They cannot stand better
    Then in her head, I think, where would you have them?
    And for her Nose, 'tis of a very good last.   70

WARD.   I have known as good as that has not lasted a year
    though.

SORDIDO.   That's in the using of a thing; will not any strong
    bridge fall down in time, if we do nothing but beat at the bottom?
    A Nose of Buff would not last always Sir, especially if it came   75
    in to th'Camp once.

WARD.   But *Sordido*, how shall we do to make her laugh, that I
    may see what Teeth she has; for I'll not bate her a tooth, nor
    take a black one into th' bargain.

SORDIDO.   Why do but you fall in talk with her, you   80
    cannot chuse but one time or other, make her laugh Sir.

WARD.   It shall go hard, but I will: Pray what qualities have you
    beside singing and dancing, can you play at Shittlecock forsooth?

ISABELLA.   I, and at Stool-ball too Sir; I have great luck at it.

WARD.   Why can you catch a Ball well?   85

ISABELLA.   I have catcht two in my lap at one game.

WARD.   What have you woman? I must have you learn
    To play at trap too, then y'are full and whole.

ISABELLA.   Any thing that you please to bring me up too,
    I shall take pains to practise.   90

WARD.   'Twill not do *Sordido*, we shall never get her mouth
    open'd wide enough.

SORDIDO.   No Sir; that's strange! then here's a trick for your
    learning.   *He yawns* ⟨*whereupon* ISABELLA *yawns too.*⟩

    Look now, look now; quick, quick there.   95

WARD.   Pox of that scurvy mannerly trick with Handkercheif,
   It hindred me a little, but I am satisfied.
   When a fair woman gapes, and stops her mouth so,
   It shows like a Cloth-stopple in a Cream-pot,
   I have fair hope of her Teeth now *Sordido*.   100
SORDIDO.   Why then y'have all well Sir, for ought I see
   She's right and straight enough, now as she stands;
   They'll commonly lie crooked, that's no matter: Wise
                                 Gamesters
   Never finde fault with that, let 'em lie still so.
WARD.   I'ld fain mark how she goes, and then I have all: For of   105
   all creatures I cannot abide a splay-footed Woman, she's an
   unlucky thing to meet in a morning; her heels keep together so,
   as if she were beginning an Irish dance still; and the wrigling of
   her Bum, playing the tune to't: But I have bethought a cleanly
   shift to finde it; dab down as you see me, and peep of one side,   110
   when her back's toward you; I'll shew you the way.
SORDIDO.   And you shall finde me apt enough to peeping,
   I have been one of them has seen mad sights
   Under your Scaffolds.
WARD.   Will it please you walk forsooth,   115
   A turn or two by your self? you are so pleasing to me,
   I take delight to view you on both sides.
ISABELLA.   I shall be glad to fetch a walk to your love Sir;
   'Twill get Affection, a good stomach Sir,
   ⟨*Aside.*⟩ Which I had need have, to fall to such course
   victuals.   120

       ⟨*She walks, while* WARD *and* SORDIDO *crouch down and*
                           look at her legs.⟩

WARD.   Now go thy ways for a clean treading Wench,
   As ever man in modesty peep't under.
SORDIDO.   I see the sweetest sight to please my Master:
   Never went Frenchman righter upon ropes
   Then she on *Florentine* rushes.   125
WARD.   'Tis enough forsooth.
ISABELLA.   And how do you like me now Sir?
WARD.   Faith so well, I never mean to part with thee Sweet-heart,
   Under some sixteen children, and all Boys.

ISABELLA.   You'll be at simple pains, if you prove kinde,   130
   And breed 'em all in your teeth.
WARD.   Nay by my Faith, what serves your belly for? 'twould
   make my cheeks look like blown Bag-pipes.

Enter GUARDIANO.

GUARDIANO.   How now Ward and Nephew,
   Gentlewoman and Neece! speak, is it so or not?   135
WARD.   'Tis so, we are both agreed Sir.
GUARDIANO.   Into your kinred then;
   There's friends, and Wine, and Musick waits to welcome you.
WARD.   Then I'll be drunk for joy.
SORDIDO.   And I for company,   140
   I cannot break my Nose in a better action.   *Exeunt.*

ACT IV

SCENE I

Enter BRANCHA *attended by two* LADIES.

BRANCHA.   HOw goes your Watches Ladies? what's a clock
   now?
FIRST LADY.   By mine full nine.
SECOND LADY.   By mine a quarter past.
FIRST LADY.   I set mine by St. *Marks.*
SECOND LADY.   St. *Anthonies* they say goes truer.   5
FIRST LADY.   That's but your opinion Madam,
   Because you love a Gentleman o'th' name.
SECOND LADY.   He's a true Gentleman then.
FIRST LADY.   So may he be
   That comes to me to night, for ought you know.   10
BRANCHA.   I'll end this strife straight: I set mine by the Sun,
   I love to set by th'best, one shall not then
   Be troubled to set often.
SECOND LADY.   You do wisely in't.
BRANCHA.   If I should set my Watch as some Girls do   15
   By ev'ry clock i'th' Town, 'twould nev'r go true;
   And too much turning of the Dials point,

Or tampring with the Spring, might in small time
Spoil the whole work too, here it wants of nine now.
FIRST LADY.   It does indeed forsooth; mine's nearest truth yet.   20
SECOND LADY.   Yet I have found her lying with an Advocate,
   which shew'd
Like two false clocks together in one Parish.
BRANCHA.   So now I thank you Ladies, I desire
   A while to be alone.
FIRST LADY.   And I am no body,   25
   Methinks, unless I have one or other with me.
   Faith my desire and hers, will nev'r be sisters.

                              Exit LADIES.

BRANCHA.   How strangely womans fortune comes about,
   This was the farthest way to come to me,
   All would have judg'd, that knew me born in *Venice*   30
   And there with many jealous eyes brought up,
   That never thought they had me sure enough,
   But when they were upon me, yet my hap
   To meet it here, so far off from my birth-place,
   My friends, or kinred, 'tis not good in sadness,   35
   To keep a maid so strict in her yong days,
   Restraint breeds wand'ring thoughts, as many fasting days
   A great desire to see flesh stirring again:
   I'll nev'r use any Girl of mine so strictly,
   How ev'r they're kept, their fortunes finde 'em out,   40
   I see't in me, if they be got in Court,
   I'll never forbid 'em the Country, nor the Court,
   Though they be born i'th' Countrey, they will come to't,
   And fetch their falls a thousand mile about,
   Where one would little think on't.   45

Enter LEANTIO ⟨*gorgeously dressed*⟩.

LEANTIO. ⟨*Aside.*⟩   I long to see how my despiser looks,
   Now she's come here to Court; these are her lodgings,
   She's simply now advanc'd: I took her out
   Of no such window, I remember first,
   That was a great deal lower, and less carv'd.   50

BRANCHA.   How now? What Silk-worm's this, i'th' name of
    pride,
    What, is it he?
LEANTIO.   A bowe i'th' ham to your greatness;
    You must have now three legs, I take it, must you not?
BRANCHA.   Then I must take another, I shall want else   55
    The service I should have; you have but two there.
LEANTIO.   Y'are richly plac'd.
BRANCHA.   Methinks y'are wond'rous brave Sir.
LEANTIO.   A sumptuous lodging.
BRANCHA.   Y'ave an excellent Suit there.   60
LEANTIO.   A Chair of Velvet.
BRANCHA.   Is your cloak lin'd through Sir?
LEANTIO.   Y'are very stately here.
BRANCHA.   Faith something proud Sir.
LEANTIO.   Stay, stay, let's see your Cloth of silver Slippers? 65
BRANCHA.   Who's your Shoomaker, h'as made you a neat Boot.
LEANTIO.   Will you have a pair,
    The Duke will lend you Spurs.
BRANCHA.   Yes, when I ride.
LEANTIO.   'Tis a brave life you lead.   70
BRANCHA.   I could nev'r see you
    In such good clothes in my time.
LEANTIO.   In your time?
BRANCHA.   Sure I think Sir
    We both thrive best asunder.   75
LEANTIO.   Y'are a whore.
BRANCHA.   Fear nothing Sir.
LEANTIO.   An impudent spightful strumpet.
BRANCHA.   Oh Sir, you give me thanks for your Captainship;
    I thought you had forgot all your good manners.   80
LEANTIO.   And to spight thee as much, look there, there read,

⟨*Shows her a letter.*⟩

Vex, gnaw, thou shalt finde there I am not love-starv'd.
The world was never yet so cold, or pitiless,
But there was ever still more charity found out,
Then at one proud fools door; and 'twere hard 'faith,   85
If I could not pass that: Read to thy shame there;

A cheerful and a beauteous Benefactor too,
As ev'r erected the good works of love.

BRANCHA. ⟨*Aside.*⟩   Lady *Livia*!
Is't possible? Her worship was my Pandress,   90
She dote, and send and give, and all to him!
Why here's a Baud plagu'd home; ⟨*To him.*⟩ y'are simply
    happy Sir,
Yet I'll not envy you.

LEANTIO.   No Court-Saint, not thou!
You keep some friend of a new fashion;   95
There's no harm in your Devil, he's a suckling,
But he will breed teeth shortly, will he not?

BRANCHA.   Take heed you play not then too long with him.

LEANTIO.   Yes, and the great one too: I shall finde time
To play a hot religious bout with some of you,   100
And perhaps drive you and your course of sins
To their eternal Kennels; I speak softly now,
'Tis manners in a noble Womans lodgings,
And I well know all my degrees of duty.
But come I to your everlasting parting once,   105
Thunder shall seem soft musick to that tempest.

BRANCHA.   'Twas said last week there would be change of
    weather,
When the Moon hung so, and belike you heard it.

LEANTIO.   Why here's sin made, and nev'r a conscience put
    to't;
A Monster with all Forehead, and no Eyes.   110
Why do I talk to thee of Sense or Vertue,
That art as dark as death? and as much madness
To set light before thee, as to lead blinde folks
To see the Monuments, which they may smell as soon
As they behold; Marry oft-times their heads   115
For want of light, may feel the hardness of 'em.
So shall thy blinde pride my revenge and anger,
That canst not see it now; and it may fall
At such an hour, when thou least seest of all;
So to an ignorance darker then thy womb,   120

IV. I. 104 know] DILKE; knew TNP.

I leave thy perjur'd soul: A plague will come.

Exit.

BRANCHA.   Get you gone first, and then I fear no greater,
　　Nor thee will I fear long; I'll have this sauciness
　　Soon banish'd from these lodgings, and the rooms
　　Perfum'd well after the corrupt air it leaves: 125
　　His breath has made me almost sick in troth,
　　A poor base start up! Life! because has got
　　Fair clothes by foul means, comes to rail, and shew 'em.

Enter the DUKE.

DUKE.   Who's that?
BRANCHA.   Cry you mercy Sir.   130
DUKE.   Prethee who's that?
BRANCHA.   The former thing my Lord, to whom you gave
　　The Captainship; he eats his meat with grudging still.
DUKE.   Still!
BRANCHA.   He comes vaunting here of his new love,   135
　　And the new clothes she gave him; Lady *Livia.*
　　Who but she now his Mistress?
DUKE.   Lady *Livia?*
　　Be sure of what you say.
BRANCHA.   He shew'd me her name Sir,   140
　　In perfum'd Paper, her Vows, her Letter,
　　With an intent to spight me; so his heart said,
　　And his threats made it good; they were as spightful
　　As ever malice utter'd, and as dangerous,
　　Should his hand follow the copy.   145
DUKE.   But that must not;
　　Do not you vex your minde, prethee to Bed, go,
　　All shall be well and quiet.
BRANCHA.   I love peace Sir.

Exit.

DUKE.   And so do all that love; take you no care for't,   150
　　It shall be still provided to your hand: Who's near us there?

Enter MESSENGER.

W.B.W.—4

MESSENGER.   My Lord.
DUKE.   Seek out *Hippolito*,
  Brother to Lady *Livia*, with all speed.
MESSENGER.   He was the last man I saw, my Lord.   155

                                                    Exit.

DUKE.   Make haste.
  He is a blood soon stir'd, and as he's quick
  To apprehend a wrong, he's bold, and sudden
  In bringing forth a ruine: I know likewise
  The reputation of his Sisters honor   160
  As dear to him as life-blood to his heart;
  Beside I'll flatter him with a goodness to her,
  Which I now thought on, but nev'r meant to practise
  (Because I know her base) and that wind drives him.
  The ulcerous reputation feels the poyse   165
  Of lightest wrongs, as sores are vext with flies:
  He comes, *Hippolito* welcome.

Enter HIPPOLITO.

HIPPOLITO.   My lov'd Lord.
DUKE.   How does that lusty Widow, thy kinde Sister;
  Is she not sped yet of a second husband?   170
  A bed-fellow she has, I ask not that,
  I know she's sped of him.
HIPPOLITO.   Of him my Lord!
DUKE.   Yes of a bed-fellow; is the news so strange to you?
HIPPOLITO.   I hope 'tis so to all.   175
DUKE.   I wish it were Sir;
  But 'tis confest too fast, her ignorant pleasures
  Onely by Lust instructed, have receiv'd
  Into their services, an impudent Boaster,
  One that does raise his glory from her shame,   180
  And tells the midday Sun, what's done in darkness;
  Yet blinded with her appetite, wastes her wealth,
  Buys her disgraces at a dearer rate,
  Then bounteous house-keepers purchase their honor.
  Nothing sads me so much, as that in love   185

IV. I. 160 honor_] ∼: T; honor's _TNPC.

To thee, and to thy blood, I had pickt out
A worthy match for her, the great *Vincentio*,
High in our favor, and in all mens thoughts.

HIPPOLITO.   Oh thou destruction of all happy fortunes,
Unsated blood! know you the name my Lord   190
Of her abuser?

DUKE.   One *Leantio*.

HIPPOLITO.   He's a Factor.

DUKE.   He nev'r made so brave a voyage by his own talk.

HIPPOLITO.   The poor old widows son;   195
I humbly take my leave.

DUKE. ⟨*Aside.*⟩   I see 'tis done:
⟨*To him.*⟩ Give her good counsel, make her see her error,
I know she'll hearken to you.

HIPPOLITO.   Yes my Lord,   200
I make no doubt, as I shall take the course,
Which she shall never know till it be acted;
And when she wakes to honor, then she'll thank me for't.
I'll imitate the pities of old Surgeons
To this lost limb, who ere they show their art,   205
Cast one asleep, then cut the diseas'd part.
So out of love to her I pity most,
She shall not feel him going till he's lost,
Then she'll commend the cure.

                                                   Exit.

DUKE.   The great cure's past;   210
I count this done already; his wrath's sure,
And speaks an injury deep; farewel *Leantio*.
This place will never hear thee murmur more.

Enter LORD CARDINAL *attended.*

Our noble Brother welcome!

LORD CARDINAL.   Set those lights down: 215
Depart till you be called.

                              ⟨*Exeunt Attendants.*⟩

DUKE.   There's serious business
Fixed in his look, nay, it enclines a little
To the dark colour of a discontentment.

Brother, what is't commands your eye so powerfully?   220
  Speak, you seem lost.
LORD CARDINAL.   The thing I look on seems so
  To my eyes lost for ever.
DUKE.   You look on me.
LORD CARDINAL.   What a grief 'tis to a religious feeling,   225
  To think a man should have a friend so goodly,
  So wise, so noble, nay, a Duke, a Brother,
  And all this certainly damn'd?
DUKE.   How!
LORD CARDINAL.   'Tis no wonder,   230
  If your great sin can do't; dare you look up
  For thinking of a veng'ance? dare you sleep
  For fear of never waking, but to death,
  And dedicate unto a strumpets love
  The strength of your affections, zeal and health?   235
  Here you stand now; can you assure your pleasures,
  You shall once more enjoy her, but once more?
  Alas you cannot; what a misery 'tis then
  To be more certain of eternal death,
  Then of a next embrace? nay, shall I shew you   240
  How more unfortunate you stand in sin,
  Then the lowe private man; all his offences,
  Like inclos'd grounds, keep but about himself,
  And seldom stretch beyond his own souls bounds;
  And when a man grows miserable, 'tis some comfort   245
  When he's no further charg'd, then with himself:
  'Tis a sweet ease to wretchedness: But great man,
  Ev'ry sin thou commit'st, shews like a flame
  Upon a Mountain, 'tis seen far about,
  And with a big wind made of popular breath,   250
  The sparkles flie through Cities: Here one takes,
  Another catches there, and in short time
  Waste all to cinders: But remember still
  What burnt the Valleys first, came from the Hill;
  Ev'ry offence draws his particular pain,   255
  But 'tis example proves the great mans bane.
  The sins of mean men, lie like scatter'd parcels

242 lowe] low DILKE; love TNP.

Of an unperfect bill; but when such fall,
Then comes example, and that sums up all:
And this your reason grants, if men of good lives,　　260
Who by their vertuous actions stir up others
To noble and religious imitation,
Receive the greater glory after death,
As sin must needs confess; what may they feel
In height of torments, and in weight of veng'ance,　　265
Not onely they themselves, not doing well,
But sets a light up to shew men to Hell?

DUKE. If you have done, I have, no more sweet Brother.

LORD CARDINAL. I know time spent in goodness, is too
tedious;
This had not been a moments space in Lust now;　　270
How dare you venture on eternal pain,
That cannot bear a minutes reprehension?
Methinks you should endure to hear that talkt of
Which you so strive to suffer. Oh my Brother!
What were you, if you were taken now,　　275
My heart weeps blood to think on't, 'tis a work
Of infinite mercy, (you can never merit)
That yet you are not death-struck, no not yet:
I dare not stay you long, for fear you should not
Have time enough allow'd you to repent in.　　280
There's but this Wall betwixt you and destruction,
When y'are at strongest, and but poor thin clay.
Think upon't Brother, can you come so near it,
For a fair strumpets love, and fall into
A torment that knows neither end nor bottom　　285
For beauty but the deepness of a skin,
And that not of their own neither: Is she a thing
Whom sickness dare not visit, or age look on,
Or death resist, does the worm shun her grave?
If not (as your soul knows it) why should Lust　　290
Bring man to lasting pain, for rotten dust?

DUKE. Brother of spotless honor, let me weep
The first of my repentance in thy bosome,
And shew the blest fruits of a thankful spirit;
And if I ere keep woman more unlawfully,　　295

May I want penitence, at my greatest need.
And wisemen know there is no barren place,
Threatens more famine, then a dearth in grace.
LORD CARDINAL.   Why here's a conversion, is at this time
   Brother
   Sung for a Himn in Heaven, and at this instant   300
   The powers of darkness groan, makes all Hell sorry.
   First, I praise Heaven, then in my work I glory.
   Who's there attends without?

Enter SERVANTS.

SERVANTS.   My Lord.
LORD CARDINAL.   Take up those lights; there was a thicker
   darkness,   305
   When they came first: the peace of a fair Soul
   Keep with my noble Brother.
DUKE.   Joys be with you Sir:

Exit LORD CARDINAL, *etc.*

She lies alone to night for't, and must still,
Though it be hard to conquer, but I have vow'd   310
Never to know her as a strumpet more,
And I must save my oath; if Fury fail not,
Her husband dies to night, or at the most,
Lives not to see the morning spent to morrow;
Then will I make her lawfully mine own,   315
Without this sin and horror. Now I'm chidden,
For what I shall enjoy then unforbidden,
And I'll not freeze in Stoves; 'tis but a while,
Live like a hopeful Bridegroom, chaste from flesh;
And pleasure then will seem new, fair and fresh.   320

                                             Exit.

                    SCENE II

                Enter HIPPOLITO.

HIPPOLITO.   The morning so far wasted, yet his baseness
   So impudent? See if the very Sun do not blush at him!

Dare he do thus much, and know me alive!
Put case one must be vitious, as I know my self
Monstrously guilty, there's a blinde time made for't;   5
He might use onely that, 'twere conscionable:
Art, silence, closeness, subtlety, and darkness,
Are fit for such a business; but there's no pity
To be bestow'd on an apparent sinner,
An impudent day-light Leacher; the great zeal   10
I bear to her advancement in this match
With Lord *Vincentio*, as the Duke has wrought it,
To the perpetual honor of our house,
Puts fire into my blood, to purge the air
Of this corruption, fear it spread too far,   15
And poyson the whole hopes of this fair fortune.
I love her good so dearly, that no Brother
Shall venture farther for a Sisters glory,
Then I for her preferment.

Enter LEANTIO, *and a* PAGE.

LEANTIO. ⟨*Aside.*⟩   Once again   20
I'll see that glistring Whore, shines like a Serpent,
Now the Court Sun's upon her: Page!
PAGE.   Anon Sir!
LEANTIO.   I'll go in state too; see the Coach be ready.
I'll hurry away presently.   25

⟨*Exit* PAGE.⟩

HIPPOLITO.   Yes you shall hurry,
And the Devil after you; take that at setting forth.

⟨*Strikes him.*⟩

Now, and you'll draw, we are upon equal terms Sir.
Thou took'st advantage of my name in honor,
Upon my Sister; I nev'r saw the stroke   30
Come, till I found my reputation bleeding;
And therefore count it I no sin to valor
To serve thy lust so: Now we are of even hand,
Take your best course against me. You must die.

IV. II. 24   I'll...ready] *Speech-allocation as in* DILKE; *in* TNP *this line is given
to the* Page.

LEANTIO.   How close sticks Envy to mans happiness?   35
When I was poor, and little car'd for life,
I had no such means offer'd me to die,
No mans wrath minded me: Slave, I turn this to thee,

⟨*Draws.*⟩

To call thee to account, for a wound lately
Of a base stamp upon me.   40
HIPPOLITO.   'Twas most fit
For a base mettle. Come and fetch one now
More noble then, for I will use thee fairer
Then thou hast done thine own soul, or our honor;

⟨*They fight.*⟩

And there I think 'tis for thee.   45

⟨LEANTIO *falls.*⟩

WITHIN.   Help, help, Oh part 'em.

LEANTIO.   False wife! I feel now th'hast praid heartily for me;
Rise Strumpet by my fall, thy Lust may raign now;
My heart-string, and the marriage knot that ty'd thee,
Breaks both together.   50

⟨*Dies.*⟩

HIPPOLITO.   There I heard the sound on't,
And never like'd string better.

Enter GUARDIANO, LIVIA, ISABELLA, WARD, *and* SORDIDO.

LIVIA.   'Tis my Brother,
Are you hurt Sir?
HIPPOLITO.   Not any thing.   55
LIVIA.   Blessed fortune,
Shift for thy self; what is he thou hast kill'd?
HIPPOLITO.   Our honors enemy.
GUARDIANO.   Know you this man Lady?
LIVIA.   *Leantio?* My loves joy? wounds stick upon thee   60
As deadly as thy sins; art thou not hurt?
The Devil take that fortune, and he dead,
Drop plagues into thy bowels without voice,
Secret, and fearful: Run for Officers,
Let him be apprehended with all speed,   65

44 thine own] DYCE; thine TNP.

For fear he scape away; lay hands on him.
We cannot be too sure, 'tis wilful murder;
You do Heavens veng'ance, and the Law just service.
You know him not as I do, he's a villain,
As monstrous as a prodigy, and as dreadful.   70

HIPPOLITO.   Will you but entertain a noble patience,
Till you but hear the reason worthy Sister!

LIVIA.   The reason! that's a jest Hell falls a laughing at:
Is there a reason found for the destruction
Of our more lawful loves? and was there none   75
To kill the black Lust twixt thy Neece and thee,
That has kept close so long?

GUARDIANO.   How's that good Madam?

LIVIA.   Too true Sir, there she stands, let her deny't;
The deed cries shortly in the Midwifes arms,   80
Unless the parents sins strike it still-born;
And if you be not deaf, and ignorant,
You'll hear strange notes ere long: Look upon me Wench!
'Twas I betray'd thy honor subtilly to him
Under a false tale; it lights upon me now;   85
His arm has paid me home upon thy breast,
My sweet belov'd _Leantio_!

GUARDIANO.   Was my judgment
And care in choice, so dev'llishly abus'd,
So beyond shamefully—All the world will grin at me.   90

WARD.   Oh _Sordido, Sordido_, I'm damn'd, I'm damn'd!

SORDIDO.   Dam'd, why Sir!

WARD.   One of the wicked; do'st not see't, a Cuckold, a plain
reprobate Cuckold.

SORDIDO.   Nay; and you be damn'd for that! be of good chear 95
Sir,
Y'have gallant company of all professions; I'll have a wife
Next Sunday too, because I'll along with you my self.

WARD.   That will be some comfort yet.

LIVIA.   You Sir, that bear your load of injuries,
As I of sorrows, lend me your griev'd strength   100
To this sad burthen; who in life wore actions,
Flames were not nimbler: We will talk of things
May have the luck to break our hearts together.

GUARDIANO.   I'll list to nothing, but revenge and anger,
Whose counsels I will follow.   105

> *Exeunt* LIVIA *and* GUARDIANO ⟨*carrying the body of*
> LEANTIO.⟩

SORDIDO.   A wife quoth'a!
Here's a sweet Plumb-tree of your Gardiner's graffing!
WARD.   Nay there's a worse name belongs to this fruit yet, and
you could hit on't, a more open one: For he that marries a whore,
looks like a fellow bound all his life time to a Medler-tree, and   110
that's good stuff; 'tis no sooner ripe, but it looks rotten; and so
do some Queans at nineteen. A pox on't, I thought there was some
knavery a broach, for something stir'd in her belly, the first night
I lay with her.
SORDIDO.   What, what Sir!   115
WARD.   This is she brought up so courtly, can sing, and dance,
and tumble too, methinks, I'll never marry wife again, that has so
many qualities.
SORDIDO.   Indeed they are seldom good Master; for likely
when they are taught so many, they will have one trick more   120
of their own finding out. Well, give me a wench but with one
good quality, to lye with none but her husband, and that's
bringing up enough for any woman breathing.
WARD.   This was the fault, when she was tend'red to me; you
never look'd to this.   125
SORDIDO.   Alas, how would you have me see through a great
Farthingal Sir! I cannot peep through a Mil-stone, or in the going,
to see what's done i'th' bottom.
WARD.   Her father prais'd her Brest, sh'ad the voice forsooth;
I marvell'd she sung so small indeed, being no Maid.   130
Now I perceive there's a yong Querister in her Belly:
This breeds a singing in my head I'm sure.
SORDIDO.   'Tis but the tune of your wives Sinquapace,
Danc'd in a Fetherbed; Faith, go lye down Master—but take
heed your Horns do not make holes in the Pillowbers.—⟨*Aside.*⟩ 135
I would not batter brows with him for a Hogshead of Angels, he
would prick my skull as full of holes as a Scriveners Sand-Box.

> *Exeunt* WARD *and* SORDIDO.

ISABELLA.   Was ever Maid so cruelly beguil'd
   To the confusion of life, soul, and honor,
   All of one womans murd'ring! I'ld fain bring   140
   Her name no nearer to my blood, then woman,
   And 'tis too much of that; Oh shame and horror!
   In that small distance from yon man to me,
   Lies sin enough to make a whole world perish.
   'Tis time we parted Sir, and left the sight   145
   Of one another, nothing can be worse
   To hurt repentance; for our very eyes
   Are far more poysonous to Religion,
   Then Basilisks to them; if any goodness
   Rest in you, hope of comforts, fear of judgments,   150
   My request is, I nev'r may see you more;
   And so I turn me from you everlastingly,
   So is my hope to miss you: but for her,
   That durst so dally with a sin so dangerous,
   And lay a snare so spightfully for my youth,   155
   If the least means but favor my revenge,
   That I may practise the like cruel cunning
   Upon her life, as she has on mine honor,
   I'll act it without pitty.
HIPPOLITO.   Here's a care   160
   Of reputation, and a Sisters fortune
   Sweetly rewarded by her: Would a silence,
   As great as that which keeps among the graves,
   Had everlastingly chain'd up her tongue;
   My love to her has made mine miserable.   165

Enter GUARDIANO *and* LIVIA ⟨*who talk together aside*⟩.

GUARDIANO.   If you can but dissemble your hearts griefs now,
   Be but a woman so far.
LIVIA.   Peace! I'll strive Sir.
GUARDIANO.   As I can wear my injuries in a smile;
   Here's an occasion offer'd, that gives anger   170
   Both liberty and safety to perform
   Things worth the fire it holds, without the fear
   Of danger, or of Law; for mischeifs acted
   Under the priviledge of a marriage-triumph

At the Dukes hasty Nuptial's, will be thought   175
Things meerly accidental; all's by chance,
Not got of their own natures.
LIVIA.   I conceive you Sir,
Even to a longing for performance on't;
And here behold some fruits.   180

⟨*Kneels to* HIPPOLITO *and* ISABELLA.⟩

Forgive me both,
What I am now return'd to Sence and Judgment,
Is not the same Rage and distraction
Presented lately to you? that rude form
Is gone for ever. I am now my self,   185
That speaks all peace, and friendship; and these tears
Are the true springs of hearty penitent sorrow
For those foul wrongs, which my forgetful fury
Sland'red your vertues with: This Gentleman
Is well resolv'd now.   190
GUARDIANO.   I was never otherways,
I knew (alas) 'twas but your anger spake it,
And I nev'r thought on't more.
HIPPOLITO.   Pray rise good Sister.
ISABELLA. ⟨*Aside.*⟩   Here's ev'n as sweet amends made for a   195
    wrong now,
As one that gives a wound, and pays the Surgeon;
All the smart's nothing, the great loss of blood,
Or time of hind'rance: Well, I had a Mother,
I can dissemble too: ⟨*To* LIVIA.⟩ What wrongs have slipt
Through angers ignorance (Aunt) my heart forgives.   200
GUARDIANO.   Why thus tuneful now!
HIPPOLITO.   And what I did Sister,
Was all for honors cause, which time to come
Will approve to you.
LIVIA.   Being awak'd to goodness,   205
I understand so much Sir, and praise now
The fortune of your arm, and of your safety;
For by his death y'have rid me of a sin
As costly as ev'r woman doted on:

182 Judgment,] judgment, DYCE; Judgment. TNP.

T'has pleas'd the Duke so well too, that (behold Sir)   210
Has sent you here your pardon, which I kist
With most affectionate comfort; when 'twas brought,
Then was my fit just past, it came so well me thought
To glad my heart.

HIPPOLITO.   I see his Grace thinks on me.   215

LIVIA.   There's no talk now but of the preparation
For the great marriage.

HIPPOLITO.   Does he marry her then?

LIVIA.   With all speed, suddenly, as fast as cost
Can be laid on with many thousand hands.   220
This Gentleman and I, had once a purpose
To have honored the first marriage of the Duke
With an invention of his own; 'twas ready
The pains well past, most of the charge bestow'd on't;
Then came the death of your good Mother (Neece)   225
And turn'd the glory of it all to black:
'Tis a device would fit these times so well too,
Art's treasury not better; if you'll joyn
It shall be done, the cost shall all be mine.

HIPPOLITO.   Y'have my voice first, 'twill well approve my   230
thankfulness
For the Dukes love and favor.

LIVIA.   What say you Neece?

ISABELLA.   I am content to make one.

GUARDIANO.   The plot's full then;
Your pages Madam, will make shift for Cupids.   235

LIVIA.   That will they Sir.

GUARDIANO.   You'll play your old part still.

LIVIA.   What is't? good troth I have ev'n forgot it.

GUARDIANO.   Why *Juno Pronuba*, the Marriage-Goddess.

LIVIA.   'Tis right indeed.   240

GUARDIANO.   ⟨*To* ISABELLA.⟩   And you shall play the Nymph,
That offers sacrifice to appease her wrath.

ISABELLA.   Sacrifice good Sir?

LIVIA.   Must I be appeased then?

---

238 What‸is't? good] ∼ is't? Good‸DILKE; ∼, is't good? TNP. *The emendation is
necessitated by Guardiano's reply. An alternative possibility is* What is't, good?;
but Middleton is not addicted to this vocative use of good.

GUARDIANO.   That's as you list your self, as you see cause.   245
LIVIA.   Methinks 'twould shew the more state in her diety,
   To be Incenst.
ISABELLA.   'Twould, but my Sacrifice
   Shall take a course to appease you, or I'll fail in't,
   ⟨*Aside.*⟩ And teach a sinful Baud to play a Goddess.   250
GUARDIANO.   For our parts, we'll not be ambitious Sir;
   Please you walk in, and see the project drawn,
   Then take your choice.
HIPPOLITO.   I weigh not, so I have one.

⟨*Exeunt all but* LIVIA.⟩

LIVIA.   How much ado have I to restrain fury   255
   From breaking into curses! Oh how painful 'tis
   To keep great sorrow smother'd! sure I think
   'Tis harder to dissemble Grief, then Love.
   Leantio, here the weight of thy loss lies,
   Which nothing but destruction can suffice.   260

Exit.

Hoboys.

SCENE III

Enter in great state the DUKE *and* BRANCHA, *richly
attir'd, with Lords, Cardinals, Ladies, and other Attendants,
they pass solemnly over: Enter* LORD CARDINAL *in a
rage, seeming to break off the Ceremony.*

LORD CARDINAL.   Cease, cease; Religious Honors done to sin,
   Disparage Vertues reverence, and will pull
   Heavens thunder upon *Florence*; holy Ceremonies
   Were made for sacred uses, not for sinful.
   Are these the fruits of your Repentance Brother?   5
   Better it had been you had never sorrow'd,
   Then to abuse the benefit, and return
   To worse then where sin left you.
   Vow'd you then never to keep Strumpet more,
   And are you now so swift in your desires,   10

To knit your honors, and your life fast to her!
Is not sin sure enough to wretched man,
But he must bind himself in chains to't? Worse!
Must marriage, that immaculate robe of honor,
That renders Vertue glorious, fair, and fruitful　　　15
To her great Master, be now made the Garment
Of Leprousie and Foulness? is this Penitence
To sanctifie hot Lust? what is it otherways
Then worship done to Devils? is this the best
Amends that sin can make after her riots?　　　20
As if a Drunkard, to appease Heavens wrath,
Should offer up his surfeit for a Sacrifice:
If that be comly, then Lust's offerings are
On Wedlocks sacred Altar.

DUKE.　　Here y'are bitter　　　25
Without cause Brother: what I vow'd I keep,
As safe as you your Conscience, and this needs not;
I taste more wrath in't, then I do Religion;
And envy more then goodness; the path now
I tread, is honest, leads to lawful love,　　　30
Which vertue in her strictness would not check:
I vow'd no more to keep a sensual woman:
'Tis done, I mean to make a lawful wife of her.

LORD CARDINAL.　　He that taught you that craft,
Call him not Master long, he will undo you:　　　35
Grow not too cunning for your soul good Brother,
Is it enough to use adulterous thefts,
And then take sanctuary in marriage?
I grant, so long as an offender keeps
Close in a priviledged Temple, his life's safe;　　　40
But if he ever venture to come out,
And so be taken, then he surely dies for't:
So now y'are safe: but when you leave this body,
Mans onely priviledg'd Temple upon Earth,
In which the guilty soul takes sanctuary,　　　45
Then you'll perceive what wrongs chaste vows endure,
When Lust usurps the Bed that should be pure.

BRANCHA.　　Sir, I have read you over all this while
In silence, and I finde great knowledge in you,

And severe learning, yet 'mongst all your vertues   50
I see not charity written, which some call
The first-born of Religion, and I wonder
I cannot see't in yours. Believe it Sir,
There is no vertue can be sooner miss'd,
Or later welcom'd; it begins the rest,   55
And sets 'em all in order; Heaven and Angels
Take great delight in a converted sinner.
Why should you then a Servant and Professor,
Differ so much from them? If ev'ry woman
That commits evil, should be therefore kept   60
Back in desires of goodness, how should vertue
Be known and honor'd? From a man that's blinde,
To take a burning Taper, 'tis no wrong,
He never misses it: But to take light
From one that see's, that's injury and spight.   65
Pray whether is Religion better serv'd,
When lives that are licentious are made honest,
Then when they still run through a sinful blood.
'Tis nothing Vertues Temples to deface;
But build the ruines, there's a work of Grace.   70

DUKE.   I kiss thee for that spirit; thou hast prais'd thy wit
A modest way: On, on there.

Hoboys.

LORD CARDINAL.   Lust is bold,
And will have veng'ance speak, er't be controld.

Exeunt.

ACT V

SCENE I

Enter GUARDIANO *and* WARD.

GUARDIANO.   SPeak, hast thou any sence of thy abuse?
Do'st thou know what wrong's done thee?
WARD.   I wear an Ass else.
I cannot wash my face, but I am feeling on't.
GUARDIANO.   Here take this Galtrop, then convey it secretly   5

Into the place I shew'd you; look you Sir,
This is the trap-door to't.

WARD.   I know't of old Uncle, since the last triumph; here rose
up a Devil with one eye I remember, with a company of fire-
works at's tail.   10

GUARDIANO.   Prethee leave squibbing now, mark me, and fail
not; but when thou hear'st me give a stamp, down with't: The
villain's caught then.

WARD.   If I miss you, hang me; I love to catch a villain, and
your stamp shall go currant I warrant you: But how shall I rise   15
up, and let him down too? All at one hole! that will be a horrible
puzzle. You know I have a part in't, I play Slander.

GUARDIANO.   True, but never make you ready for't.

WARD.   No, my clothes are bought and all, and a foul Fiends head
with a long contumelious tongue i'th' chaps on't, a very fit shape   20
for Slander i'th' out-parishes.

GUARDIANO.   It shall not come so far, thou understandst it not.

WARD.   Oh, oh!

GUARDIANO.   He shall lie deep enough ere that time,
And stick first upon those.   25

WARD.   Now I conceive you Gardiner.

GUARDIANO.   Away, list to the privy stamp, that's all thy part.

WARD.   Stamp my Horns in a Morter if I miss you, and give the
powder in White-wine to sick Cuckolds, a very present remedy
for the head-ach.   30

Exit WARD.

GUARDIANO.   If this should any way miscarry now,
As if the fool be nimble enough, 'tis certain,
The Pages that present the swift wing'd *Cupids*,
Are taught to hit him with their shafts of love,
Fitting his part, which I have cunningly poyson'd;   35
He cannot 'scape my fury; and those ills
Will be laid all on Fortune, not our Wills,
That's all the sport on't; for who will imagine,
That at the celebration of this night
Any mischance that hap's, can flow from spight?   40

Exit.

Florish.

SCENE II

Enter above, DUKE, BRANCHA, LORD CARDINAL,
FABRITIO, *and other Cardinals, Lords and Ladies in State.*

DUKE.   Now our fair Dutchess, your delight shall witness,
How y'are belov'd and honor'd; all the glories
Bestow'd upon the gladness of this night,
Are done for your bright sake.
BRANCHA.   I am the more   5
In debt my Lord, to loves and curtesies,
That offer up themselves so bounteously
To do me honor'd Grace, without my merit.
DUKE.   A goodness set in greatness; how it sparkles
Afar off like pure Diamonds set in Gold!   10
How perfect my desires were, might I witness
But a fair noble peace, 'twixt your two spirits!
The reconcilement would be more sweet to me,
Then longer life to him that fears to die.
Good Sir!   15
LORD CARDINAL.   I profess Peace, and am content.
DUKE.   I'll see the Seal upon't, and then 'tis firm.
LORD CARDINAL.   You shall have all you wish.

⟨*Kisses* BRANCHA.⟩

DUKE.   I have all indeed now.
BRANCHA. ⟨*Aside.*⟩   But I have made surer work; this shall not   20
blinde me;
He that begins so early to reprove,
Quickly rid him, or look for little love;
Beware a Brothers envy, he's next heir too.
Cardinal you die this night, the plot's laid surely:
In time of sports Death may steal in securely;   25
Then 'tis least thought on:
For he that's most religious, holy Friend,
Does not at all hours think upon his end;
He has his times of frailty, and his thoughts
Their transportations too, through flesh and blood,   30

For all his zeal, his learning, and his light,
As well as we, poor soul, that sin by night.

⟨FABRITIO *gives a paper to the* DUKE.⟩

DUKE.   What's this *Fabritio?*
FABRITIO.   Marry, my Lord, the model
Of what's presented.   35
DUKE.   Oh we thank their loves;
Sweet Dutchess take your seat, list to the Argument.

Reads.

T*Here is a Nymph that haunts the Woods and Springs,*
In love with two at once, and they with her;
Equal it runs; but to decide these things,   40
The cause to mighty Juno *they refer,*
She being the Marriage-Goddess; the two Lovers
They offer sighs, the Nymph a Sacrifice,
All to please Juno, *who by signs discovers,*
How the event shall be, so that strife dies: 45
Then springs a second; for the man refus'd
Grows discontent, and out of love abus'd,
He raises Slander *up, like a black Fiend,*
To disgrace th'other, which pays him i'th' end?
BRANCHA.   In troth, my Lord, a pretty pleasing Argument,   50
And fits th'occasion well; *Envy* and *Slander*
Are things soon rais'd against two faithful Lovers;
But comfort is, they are not long unrewarded.

Musick.

DUKE.   This musick shews they're upon entrance now.
BRANCHA. ⟨*Aside.*⟩   Then enter all my wishes.   55

Enter HYMEN *in Yellow,* GANYMED *in a Blue robe powdered with
Stars, and* HEBE *in a White robe with golden Stars, with covered
Cups in their hands: They dance a short dance, then bowing to the*
DUKE, *etc.* HYMEN *speaks.*

HYMEN.   To thee fair Bride *Hymen* offers up
Of nuptial joys this the Celestial Cup.

Taste it, and thou shalt ever finde
Love in thy Bed, peace in thy minde.

⟨*Gives a cup to* BRANCHA.⟩

BRANCHA.   We'll taste you sure, 'twere pitty to disgrace   60
So pretty a beginning.

⟨*Drinks from the cup.*⟩

DUKE.   'Twas spoke nobly.
GANYMED.   Two Cups of *Nectar* have we begg'd from *Jove*;
Hebe give that to Innocence, I this to love.

⟨HEBE *gives a cup to the* LORD CARDINAL, *and*
GANYMED *a cup to the* DUKE: *they drink*⟩.

Take heed of stumbling more, look to your way;   65
Remember still the *Via Lactea*.
HEBE.   Well *Ganymed*, you have more faults, though not so
known;
I spil'd one Cup, but you have filtch'd many a one.
HYMEN.   No more, forbear for *Hymens* sake;
In love we met, and so let's part.   70

Exeunt ⟨HYMEN, GANYMED, *and* HEBE⟩.

DUKE.   But soft! here's no such persons in the Argument,
As these three, *Hymen, Hebe, Ganymed*.
The Actors that this model here discovers,
Are onely four, *Juno*, a Nymph, two Lovers.
BRANCHA.   This is some Antemask belike, my Lord,   75
To entertain time; ⟨*Aside.*⟩ now my peace is perfect.
⟨*To him.*⟩ Let sports come on a pace, now is their time, my
Lord:

Musick.

Hark you, you hear from 'em!
DUKE.   The Nymph indeed.

Enter two drest like Nymphs, bearing two Tapers lighted; then
ISABELLA *drest with flowers and Garlands, bearing a Censor with*
fire in it; they set the Censor and Tapers on Juno's *Altar with*
much reverence; this Ditty being sung in parts.

Ditty.

JUno *Nuptial-Goddess, thou that rul'st o'r coupled bodies,*   80

Ty'st man to woman, never to forsake her, thou onely powerful
marriage-maker,
Pitty this amaz'd affection; I love both, and both love me,
Nor know I where to give rejection, my heart likes so equally,
Till thou set'st right my Peace of life,
And with thy power conclude this strife.   85

ISABELLA.   Now with my thanks depart you to the Springs;

⟨*Exeunt Nymphs.*⟩

I to these Wells of Love: Thou sacred Goddess,
And Queen of Nuptials, Daughter to great *Saturn*,
Sister and Wife to *Jove*, Imperial *Juno*,
Pitty this passionate conflict in my Brest,   90
This tedious War, 'twixt two Affections;
Crown one with victory, and my heart's at peace.

Enter HIPPOLITO *and* GUARDIANO, *like Shepherds.*

HIPPOLITO.   Make me that happy man, thou mighty Goddess.
GUARDIANO.   But I live most in hope, if truest love
   Merit the greatest comfort.   95
ISABELLA.   I love both
   With such an even and fair affection,
   I know not which to speak for, which to wish for,
   Till thou great Arbitress, 'twixt lovers hearts,
   By thy auspicious Grace, design the man;   100
   Which pitty I implore.
BOTH.   We all implore it.

LIVIA *descends like* Juno ⟨*attended by Cupids*⟩.

ISABELLA.   And after sighs, contritions truest odors,
   I offer to thy powerful Deity,
   This precious Incense, may it ascend peacefully;   105
   ⟨*Aside.*⟩ And if it keep true touch, my good Aunt *Juno*,
   'Twill try your immortality er't be long:
   I fear you'll never get so nigh Heaven again,
   When you're once down.
LIVIA.   Though you and your affections   110
   Seem all as dark to our illustrious brightness

v. II. 92 one] MULRYNE; me TNP.
   107 be long] DILKE; belong TNP.

As nights inheritance Hell, we pitty you,
And your requests are granted: You ask signs;
They shall be given you, we'll be gracious to you.
He of those twain which we determine for you,   115
Loves Arrows shall wound twice, the later wound
Betokens love in age; for so are all
Whose love continues firmly all their life time,
Twice wounded at their marriage; else affection
Dies when youth ends: ⟨*Aside.*⟩ This savor overcomes me.   120
⟨*Aloud.*⟩ Now for a sign of wealth and golden days,
Bright-ey'd Prosperity, which all couples love,
I, and makes love take that: Our Brother *Jove*
Never denies us of his burning treasure,
T'express bounty.   125

⟨LIVIA *throws down* "*treasure*" *to* ISABELLA, *who falls and
dies.*⟩

DUKE.   She falls down upon't,
  What's the conceit of that?
FABRITIO.   As over-joy'd belike:
  Too much prosperity overjoyes us all,
  And she has her lapful, it seems my Lord.   130
DUKE.   This swerves a little from the Argument though: Look
  you my Lords.
GUARDIANO. ⟨*Aside.*⟩   All's fast; now comes my part to toll
  him hither;
  Then with a stamp given, he's dispatch'd as cunningly.
HIPPOLITO.   Stark dead: Oh treachery! cruelly made away!
  how's that?

⟨GUARDIANO *falls through the trap-door.*⟩

FABRITIO.   Look, there's one of the Lovers dropt away too.   135
DUKE.   Why sure this plot's drawn false, here's no such thing.
LIVIA.   Oh I am sick to th' death, let me down quickly;
  This fume is deadly: Oh 't'has poyson'd me!

---

120 savor] savour DILKE; favor TNP. *The original reading would make sense if the
sentence were transferred to Isabella. But the substitution of "ſ" for "long s" can
easily occur by foul case, and seems the more likely mistake.*

My subtilty is sped, her art h'as quitted me;
My own ambition pulls me down to ruine.   140

⟨Falls and dies.⟩

HIPPOLITO.   Nay, then I kiss thy cold lips, and applaud
This thy revenge in death.

⟨Kisses the dead ISABELLA.⟩

FABRITIO.   Look, *Juno*'s down too:

Cupids shoot ⟨and hit HIPPOLITO⟩.

What makes she there? her pride should keep aloft.
She was wont to scorn the Earth in other shows: 145
Methinks her Peacocks Feathers are much pull'd.
HIPPOLITO.   Oh death runs through my blood; in a wilde
flame too:
Plague of those *Cupids*; some lay hold on 'em.
Let 'em not 'scape, they have spoil'd me; the shaft's deadly.
DUKE.   I have lost my self in this quite.   150
HIPPOLITO.   My great Lords, we are all confounded.
DUKE.   How?
HIPPOLITO.   Dead; and I worse.
FABRITIO.   Dead? my Girl dead? I hope
My Sister *Juno* has not serv'd me so.   155
HIPPOLITO.   Lust, and forgetfulness has been amongst us,
And we are brought to nothing: Some blest Charity
Lend me the speeding Pitty of his Sword
To quench this fire in blood. *Leantio*'s death
Has brought all this upon us; now I taste it,   160
And made us lay plots to confound each other;
The event so proves it, and mans understanding
Is riper at his fall, then all his life time.
She in a madness for her lovers death,
Reveal'd a fearful Lust in our near bloods,   165
For which I am punish'd dreadfully and unlook'd for;
Prov'd her own ruine too, Veng'ance met Vengeance,
Like a set match; as if the plague of sin
Had been agreed to meet here altogether.
But how her fawning partner fell, I reach not,   170

Unless caught by some spring of his own setting:
(For on my pain, he never dream'd of dying)
The plot was all his own, and he had cunning
Enough to save himself; but 'tis the property
Of guilty deeds to draw your wisemen downward.   175
Therefore the wonder ceases.—Oh this torment!
DUKE.   Our Guard below there!

Enter a LORD *with a Guard.*

LORD.   My Lord.
HIPPOLITO.   Run and meet death then,
And cut off time and pain.   180

⟨*Kills himself by running on a guard's weapon.*⟩

LORD.   Behold my Lord, h'as run his Brest upon a weapons
point.
DUKE.   Upon the first night of our nuptial honors,
Destruction play her triumph, and great mischiefs
Mask in expected pleasures, 'tis prodigious!
They're things most fearfully ominous: I like 'em not.   185
Remove these ruin'd bodies from our eyes.

⟨*The Guard carry off the dead bodies.*⟩

BRANCHA. ⟨*Aside.*⟩   Not yet, no change? when falls he to the
Earth?
LORD.   Please but your Excellence to peruse that Paper,
Which is a brief confession from the heart
Of him that fell first, ere his soul departed;   190
And there the darkness of these deeds speaks plainly.
'Tis the full scope, the manner, and intent;
His Ward, that ignorantly let him down,
Fear put to present flight at the voice of him.
BRANCHA. ⟨*Aside.*⟩   Nor yet?   195
DUKE.   Read, read; for I am lost in sight and strength.

⟨*Falls.*⟩

LORD CARDINAL.   My noble Brother!
BRANCHA.   Oh the curse of wretchedness!
My deadly hand is faln upon my Lord:

Destruction take me to thee, give me way; 200
The pains and plagues of a lost soul upon him,
That hinders me a moment.

DUKE. My heart swells bigger yet; help here, break't ope,
My brest flies open next.

BRANCHA. Oh with the poyson, 205
That was prepar'd for thee, thee, Cardinal!
'Twas meant for thee.

LORD CARDINAL. Poor Prince!

BRANCHA. Accursed Error!
Give me thy last breath, thou infected bosome, 210
And wrap two spirits, in one poyson'd vapor.
Thus, thus, reward thy murderer, and turn death
Into a parting kiss:

⟨*Kisses him. He dies.*⟩

My soul stands ready at my lips,
Ev'n vext to stay one minute after thee. 215

LORD CARDINAL. The greatest sorrow and astonishment
That ever struck the general peace of *Florence*,
Dwells in this hour.

BRANCHA. So my desires are satisfied,
I feel deaths power within me. 220
Thou hast prevail'd in something (cursed poyson)
Though thy cheif force was spent in my Lords bosom;
But my deformity in spirit's more foul;
A blemish'd face best fits a leprous soul.
What make I here? these are all strangers to me, 225
Not known but by their malice; now th'art gone;
Nor do I seek their pities.

⟨*Drinks from the poisoned cup.*⟩

LORD CARDINAL. O restrain
Her ignorant wilful hand!

BRANCHA. Now do; 'tis done. 230
Leantio. Now I feel the breach of marriage
At my heart-breaking: Oh the deadly snares
That Women set for Women, without pity
Either to soul or honor! Learn by me

To know your foes: In this belief I die;   235
Like our own Sex, we have no Enemy, no Enemy!
LORD.   See my Lord
What shift sh'as made to be her own destruction.
BRANCHA.   Pride, Greatness, Honors, Beauty, Youth,
Ambition,
You must all down together, there's no help for't: 240
Yet this my gladness is, that I remove,
Tasting the same death in a cup of love.

⟨*Dies.*⟩

LORD CARDINAL.   Sin, what thou art, these ruines show too
piteously.
Two Kings on one Throne cannot sit together,
But one must needs down, for his Titles wrong;   245
So where lust raigns, that Prince cannot raign long.

Exeunt.

FINIS.

TEXTUAL NOTES

SIGLA

TNP = *Two New Playes* (1657)

TNPc = *Two New Playes* (1657) corrected.

L = Copy of TNP in British Museum (643.b.37).

VI = Copy of TNP in Victoria and Albert Museum (6567.17.P.28).

V2 = Another copy of TNP in Victoria and Albert Museum (6567.17.P.29).

O = Copy in the Bodleian Library (Malone 247).

T = Copy in Trinity College Library, Cambridge.

W = Copy in Worcester College Library, Oxford.

DILKE = *Old Plays; Being a Continuation of Dodsley's Collection*, vol. 5, [ed. C. W. Dilke]. London 1816.

DYCE = *The Works of Thomas Middleton*, in 5 vols., ed. Alexander Dyce. London 1840.

BULLEN = *The Works of Thomas Middleton*, in 8 vols., ed. A. H. Bullen. London 1885–6.

SIMPSON = Percy Simpson, "Thomas Middleton's 'Women Beware Women'", in *M.L.R.*, XXXIII (1938), pp. 45–6.

JACOBS = Elizabeth R. Jacobs, *A Critical Edition of Thomas Middleton's WOMEN BEWARE WOMEN*. An unpublished thesis, University of Wisconsin, 1941.

MULRYNE = J. R. Mulryne, *A Critical Edition of Thomas Middleton's "Women Beware Women"*. An unpublished thesis, University of Cambridge, 1962.

The caret mark ʌ is used throughout the Notes to indicate the absence of punctuation; the wavy dash ~ denotes the exact repetition of a word given in the lemma.

I. I

ACT I/SCENE I] Act 1. Scæn. 1. TNP.

4 gladness,] DILKE; ~. TNP.

44 mine,] TNPc; mineʌ O, T, W.

67 done] DILKE; doue TNP.

83 year,] TNPc; ~; L, VI, V2.

87 (Mother). As] ~ʌ As TNP.

I. II

SCENE II] Scæn. 2. TNP.
28   her;] DILKE; ∼, TNP.
28   me,] DILKE; ∼; TNP.
30   widow,] DILKE; ∼. TNP.
37   Counting] DILKE; Connting TNP.
89   ISABELLA.] *Isab.* DILKE; *Neece.* TNP. *Throughout this scene,* TNP *uses the speech-prefix* Neece., *but in all later scenes it is invariably* Isab. .
98   S.D. *Enter*] *This is the first word on* HI; *but the catchword on* G8v *is* Scæn. .
131 do't.] TNPC; JACOBS *reports* do't: *as the reading of the Library of Congress copy.*
138 exercise∧] TNPC; ∼, *Library of Congress copy* (MULRYNE).
143 nev'r a] nev'ra TNP.
146 Sir?] TNPC; JACOBS *reports* Sir, *as the reading of the Library of Congress copy.*
186 it.] TNPC; ∼, *Library of Congress copy* (MULRYNE).

I. III

SCENE III] Scæn. 3. TNP.
14   me,] me∧ TNP.
26   full] DILKE; sull TNP.
50   peace.] DILKE; ∼∧ TNP.
55   double.] DILKE; ∼∧ TNP.
78   S.D. SECOND BOY.] 2 *Boy.* DILKE; 2. TNP.
79   S.D. THIRD BOY.] 3 *Boy.* DILKE; 3. TNP.
81   S.D. FIRST BOY.] I *Boy.* TNP.
117 S.D. CARDINAL,] *Cardinal,* TNPC; JACOBS *reports* Cardinal∧ *as the reading of the Library of Congress copy.*
118 How . . .] *This is the first line of* H5v, *which is page* 106 *(and so numbered in* TNPC*)*: JACOBS *reports that the Library of Congress copy incorrectly numbers it* 306.

II. I

ACT II/SCENE I] Act. 2. Scæn. I. TNP.
65   the works] JACOBS; theworks TNP.
65   S.D. *Enter* SERVANT] *Placed after line* 66 *in* TNP, 65 *and* 66 *forming a single line.*
85   S.D. *Enter . . . Neece*] *Paced after line* 88 *in* TNP, 85 *and* 86 *forming a single line.*
126 Virgin—] virgin— DILKE; Virgin: TNP.
140 Fathers∧] TNPC; JACOBS *reports* Fathers, *as the reading of the Library of Congress copy.*
204 S.D. *Enter* HIPPOLITO] *Placed after line* 205 *in* TNP, 204 *and* 205 *forming a single line.*
242 now,] O; ∼; TNPC.
257 Love] TNPC; love O.
      Sir,] O; ∼; TNPC.
263 her∧] TNPC; ∼, O.
265 Art] TNPC; art O.

II. II

SCENE II] Scæn. 2. TNP.
9   window,] O; ∼; TNPC.
17   folly,] O; ∼; TNPC.
23   heart:] O; ∼! TNPC.
29   standing,] DILKE; ∼. TNP.
50   three] DILKE; theee TNP.
50   S.D. *Enter* FABRITIO] *Placed after line* 51 *in* TNP, 50 *and* 51 *forming a single line.*
89   vain] O; vein TNPC.
95   heir.] O; ∼! TNPC.
102 Ward,] TNPC; ∼∧ O.
105 ask'd] DILKE; ask TNP.
105 any where] O; anywhere TNPC.
107 Herb-woman,] O; ∼∧ TNPC.
180 'Mongst] DILKE; ,Mongst TNP.
204 evening,] O; ∼! TNPC.
206 evening!] MULRYNE; ∼∧ TNP. *The proof-reader marked an exclamation-point to be inserted here, but*

the compositor mistakenly inserted it after evening *in line 204.*

213 hearts-ease?] TNPC; ~. O.
227 request_∧] O; ~? TNPC.
232 now_∧] TNPC; ~, O.
240 truth,] O; ~; TNPC.
283 respect] TNPC; JACOBS *reports* refpect *as the reading of the Texas and Harvard copies.*
308 forsooth] DILKE; forfooth TNP.
341 well—] DILKE; ~, TNP.
358 Simplicitie] TNPC; Simplicities O.
387 here] DILKE; here's TNP.
551 S.D. Exeunt] *Placed after line 550 in* TNP.

III. I

ACT III/SCENE I] Act. 3. Scæn. I. TNP.

21 gilt casting-Bottle] gilt casting-bottle DYCE; gilt-casting Bottle TNP.
25 sleeps—] ~: TNP.
41 good] *good* DILKE; gook TNP.
65 a whit] DILKE; awhit TNP.
154 'tis] DILKE; 'till TNP.
212 too,] *the punctuation-mark in* TNP *is undecipherable.*
303 Handkerchiefs] handkerchiefs DILKE; Handerchiefs TNP.

III. II

S.D. SCENE II] Scæn_∧ 2. TNP (*but with catchword* Scæn.).
46 Suppli'd] JACOBS; Suppli' TNP.
104 hard-conscienc'd_∧ worldling] DYCE; hard_∧ conscienc'd-worldling TNP.
173–6 Here's . . . kitlings] *In* TNP, *the page is divided into two columns and this speech is placed alongside the Song, to show that the Ward speaks it while Isabella is singing.*
196 entreat] DILKE; en reat TNP.
307 Sir—] ~: TNP.
382 must] DILKE; mnst TNP.

408 abundantly] DILKE; abundantfy TNP.
411 so.] DILKE; so_∧ TNP.

III. III

S.D. SCENE III] Scæn_∧ 3. TNP.
6 courtly] DILKE; conrtly TNP.
10 choice),] choice)_∧ TNP.
59 by,] TNPC; by; T.
67 well?] TNPC; well. T.
74 bottom?] TNPC; ~: T.
79 th'] T; th TNPC. *The apostrophe probably dropped out when the compositor corrected the punctuation in lines 83 and 96.*
83 dancing,] T; ~? TNPC.
96 Handkercheif,] T; ~; TNPC.
108 the] DILKE; he TNP.

IV. I

ACT IV/SCENE I] Act. 4. Scæn. I. TNP.

27 S.D. Exit] T; Exeunt TNPC.
32 enough,] TNPC; ~; T.
33 me,] T; ~; TNPC.
35 kinred,] T; ~; TNPC.
36 days,] T; ~; TNPC.
41 me,] T; ~; TNPC.
62 Sir?] TNPC; ~. T.
65 Slippers?] T; ~; TNPC.
66 Shoomaker,] T; ~? TNPC.
67 pair,] T; ~? TNPC.
147 go,] TNPC; ~_∧ T.
151 there?] TNPC; ~. T.
163 practise_∧] MULRYNE; ~. TNP.
165 poyse_∧] TNPC; ~, T.
166 Of] TNPC; If T.
169 Sister;] T; ~? TNPC.
173 Lord!] TNPC; ~: T.
177 fast,] T; ~; TNPC.
213 S.D. Enter . . .] *In* TNP *this stage-direction is placed after line* 214.
268 done,] T; ~_∧ TNPC.
272 minutes] TNPC; minuts T.
275 now,] T; ~! TNPC.
276 on't,] T; ~; TNPC.

283 Brother,] T; ~; TNPC.
286 beauty‸] TNPC; ~; T.
287 neither:] T; ~? TNPC.
289 resist,] T; ~? TNPC.
297 place,] T; ~‸ TNPC.
299 conversion,] T; ~‸ TNPC.
300 Himn] T; Hymn TNPC.
304 Lord.] ~: T; ~! TNPC.
308 S.D. *Exit . . .*] *In* TNP *this* S.D. *is
     placed after line* 307.

IV. II

     S.D. SCENE II] Scæn‸ 2. TNP.
94   reprobate] DILKE; rebrobate TNP.
170 gives] DILKE; g ves TNP.
173 mischeifs] mischiefs DILKE; mis-
     cheif's TNP.
180–1 And . . . both] *A single line of
       verse in* TNP.
187 sorrow] DILKE; sorrow j TNP.
254 S.D. *Exeunt . . .* LIVIA] *Exit* TNP.

260 S.D. *Exit*] DILKE; *Exeunt* TNP.

IV. III

     S.D. SCENE III] Scæn‸ 3. TNP.

V. I

ACT V/SCENE I] Act. 5. Scæn. 1.
TNP.

V. II

     S.D. SCENE II] Scæn‸ 2. TNP.
26   Then] DILKE; then TNP. *In* TNP,
     25 *and* 26 *form a single line of
     verse.*
80   JUno] IUno TNP. *The only
     example in* TNP *of* i *used conson-
     antally instead of* j.
103 contritions‸] DILKE; ~, TNP.
127 What's] DILKE; Whas's TNP.
213–14 Into . . . lips]; *a single line of
        verse in* TNP.

COMMENTARY

Shakespeare line-references are to the one-volume edition of Peter Alexander. Glasgow (Collins) 1951. Dobson = E. J. Dobson, *English Pronunciation 1500–1700*. Oxford (Clarendon Press) 1957.

DRAMATIS PERSONAE

Brancha] This is the invariable spelling of the 1657 edition. Dyce, followed by later editors, emended it to *Bianca*, because (*a*) the historical character was Bianca Capello, and (*b*) the metre often seems to demand a trisyllabic form. The first reason is not compelling: Jacobean dramatists do not always reproduce foreign names accurately; and in any case we do not know Middleton's immediate source for the story—and *Branca* is the Portuguese name corresponding to Italian *Bianca*. The second reason is more persuasive, and there are certainly about a dozen lines that flow more smoothly if we accept the emendation. But in fact that is a concealed circularity in the argument: our ideas of Middleton's metre tend to be based on Dyce, or on editions derived from his (*e.g.* Bullen, the Mermaid), and in these editions there are numerous small emendations aimed at making the rhythm smoother and the line-length more regular; so that the metrical criteria that we apply to the Brancha/Bianca problem are probably those of the editors rather than of Middleton himself. The metrical argument for *Bianca* may well be sound: but before it is accepted we

need a complete analysis of Middleton's metrical habits, based, not on Dyce, but on the original editions. In the meantime, it seems reasonable to give modern readers a chance to find out what it is like to read the play with the name in the 1657 form. It is worth adding that, in Middleton's own handwriting, *Bi* is clearly distinct from *Br* (and *bi* from *br*), and misreading is unlikely. (Mulryne therefore emends to *Beancha*.)

I. I

Although there are three characters in this scene, they never converse together: the scene is constructed on *pairs* of characters, the third always standing apart. Leantio and Brancha enter together, while Leantio's mother enters by a different door, but Leantio immediately goes to his mother and converses with her, unheard by Brancha. For well over 100 lines Brancha is left standing silent, something for the audience to wonder about. Then the Mother moves to Brancha and talks with her while Leantio stands apart making comments aside. Then Brancha moves to Leantio for a brief kissing-scene, while the Mother is silent. Finally the Mother takes Brancha into the house, leaving Leantio to end the scene with a soliloquy. The whole thing has a very formal, patterned quality in its groupings.

5   her curse of sorrows] In child-birth. See *Genesis* III. 16.

22 a white sheet] The winding-sheet for a corpse.

33 Now] The implication is that formerly it has been otherwise. One of the many indications in the play that Leantio has been a ladies' man.

49 keep councel] "keep it secret".

76 flowing to affections, wills, and humors] *Flowing* could mean "rising like the tide" or "overflowing"; *affection* is "inclination, bent" or "passion, lust", and *will* perhaps "desire, appetite".

79 mar all . . . marvel] Perhaps a pun: in familiar speech, *marvel* was often pronounced *marl*.

110 because they are perfit] "Because they themselves are completely accomplished in the sport."

159 turn up the Glass] *i.e.* turn the hour-glass over.

I. II

53 blown man] Simpson proposes the emendation *blown woman*; but *man* is presumably a vocative.

64 Light her now] This is obscure; one could expect it to mean something like "Give her best", but no such meaning is recorded. Bullen conjectures *Like enow*, but this implies a purely aural mistake, and so is implausible either for a scribe or for a compositor. Simpson suggests *Plight her now* (referring to Isabella), but this gives a very abrupt transition. Jacobs takes *Light* as equivalent to *Light on*, and paraphrases "Come back at her now if you can". Mulryne paraphrases "Let her come in now".

64 Brother] It is clear from many things that Guardiano lives at Livia's house. Later, he calls Isabella "Neece" (III. III. 135), before she has married his nephew. It seems likely that Middleton imagined him as Livia's brother-in-law (brother to her dead husband), and therefore "brother" to Fabritio.

75 walk in 'em] *i.e.* walk in their sleep.

90 tongues] *i.e.* what people say.

97 here's a foul great peece] Presumably a part of the Ward's anatomy here appears on stage.

104 Jacks] Presumably some real person known to the original audience.

117 lose a fair end] Probably "lose an advantage"; *end* was also a technical term for a definite portion of certain games, but *O.E.D.* does not record an instance in this sense before 1688.

132 I'm dog at a hole] *To be dog at* meant "to be adept at, experienced in". *A hole* may refer to the game called Hole or Troll-madam, in which balls were rolled through arches (here with a sexual meaning).

140 A Cock-horse] "Astride, mounted", but here "sexually aroused".

142 Eggs in Moon-shine nights] Presumably the same as *eggs in moonshine*, *i.e.* "poached eggs".

154 out of your liberty] "Outside the area of your jurisdiction."

181 You see my honesty] He is still addressing his sorrows; they would befriend him by killing him.

204 four warring Elements] According to the traditional physics, the universe was composed of four qualities, Hot, Cold, Dry, and Moist. These combined in pairs to form the four Elements (Earth, Water, Air, Fire), and in man the

corresponding four Humours (Melancholy, Phlegm, Blood, Choler). In Chaos, the Elements were in a state of perpetual warfare, but in the universe had been brought into harmony by the Creator. Middleton is here echoing Marlowe: "Nature that fram'd vs of foure Elements, / Warring within our breasts for regiment" (*Tamburlaine* Part I, 869–70).

248 welcome it] Ironical: "Do you imagine that I could welcome this news?"

255–6 come ... doom] A rhyme. There was a variant pronunciation of *come* with ME vowel-lengthening: see Dobson p. 490.

I. III

8–9 stick Fast in their fingers ends] And so prevent them from working efficiently; a proverbial phrase. *Heads* means "people".

20 a match] "agreed".

21 Oh fie . . .] In the lines that follow, Leantio shows more strength of character than anywhere else in the play, and it is ironical that this departure should be one of the circumstances that makes Brancha's seduction possible.

24 Fondness is but the Idiot to Affection] "Infatuation is an idiot compared to Love", or perhaps "Folly is Lust's jester (*i.e.* attendant)".

25 Hot-cockles] A rustic game in which one player is blindfolded and has to guess who strikes him. Here the context gives it a sexual meaning.

27 cracks] *i.e.* is full to bursting.

55 I never ... double] He had always had a pillion-rider, *i.e.* had never lacked a girl-friend.

59 not care which end goes forward] "be negligent" (proverbial).

73 But ... Fountain] *It* is Love, and *her face* is the face of the girl who is in love. *In a Fountain* means both "in tears" and "reflected in a fountain".

75 By a dish of water] *i.e.* using it as a mirror.

117 s.d. *Enter* ...] One of the participants in this procession is Guardiano, to whom the Duke points out Brancha at the window (see II. II. 1–20). When the procession goes off, it is presumably followed by the spectators below (citizens, boys).

II. I

9 turn thy point to thine own blood] "cause you to have sexual desire for a blood-relative".

14–18 It is ... stock] *Stranger* means (*a*) "somebody not a blood-relation" and (*b*) "visitor, somebody to whom hospitality is offered". A great man had to be generous and keep open house, and would not thank his servants for being niggardly. Similarly, the man who "spares free means" (*i.e.* does not accept what is generously offered to him gratis), but uses his own goods instead, seems to scorn the bounty of God. Hippolito is doing this by neglecting the women that Heaven has bountifully made available for him, and by loving Isabella instead; *stock* carries the double meaning of "goods, capital" and "family, kin".

19 sow'd up] *i.e.* "sewn up". This was commonly used of surgical stitching, and Hippolito is saying bitterly "How quickly you have cured my wound, by telling the

truth about it!". *Counting* probably means "recounting, narrating".

51–2   You are . . . be] A mixture of two constructions: (*a*) "You are not the first who has attempted this (*or* things as forbidden as this)", and (*b*) "People have attempted things more forbidden than this".

81   none] *i.e.* no pity.

105   of force] "perforce, necessarily".

119   'twixt mine eye lids] Presumably means "in my head".

167   Marquess of *Coria*] This name occurs in the source-material, but there is nothing to show which holder of the title is meant. The Marquisate had been established by Henry IV of Castile in 1465, and was one of the titles of the dukes of Alva.

190   the great Canopy] *i.e.* the sky.

258   Though you be one] *Viz.* "a stranger" (not a blood-relative).

II. II

4–5   Sunday-dinner . . . thursday Supper-woman] The Mother is one of the poor neighbours of the great house, invited as a matter of routine and on undistinguished occasions.

23   strangly] This might represent either *strongly* or *strangely*, but, in view of the high frequency in the play of *strange* and its derivatives, is almost certainly *strangely*. See Critical Introduction, p. 6.

50   Court Passage with three Dice in a Dish] *Passage* means (*a*) transaction, (*b*) amorous encounter, (*c*) a gambling game for two people played with three dice. There is plainly a coarse sexual meaning in *three Dice in a Dish*.

92   neerer] "more closely related".

106   ask her in a Congregation] *i.e.* have the banns published in church (so that no licence would be necessary).

120–1   long . . . tongue] For the rhyme, see Dobson pp. 583–4, 590–2.

140   if I finde her naked on Record] "if I find in the ancient records that she ought to be naked".

168   When business . . . home] One of the many things that shows that Guardiano is imagined as living in Livia's house.

230   your men] *i.e.* your chess-men.

304   men enough to part you] *i.e.* the chess-men, which of course are between Livia and the Mother.

336   there came a paltry Rook] From this point, everything said about the game of chess has, for Livia and for the audience, a double meaning, referring to the seduction being enacted above.

339   the game] For the audience, this carries something of its cant meaning, "prostitution".

347   Duke] Rook (in chess).

395–7   The lifting . . . rais'd him] This hinges on the double meaning of *exalt* ("praise" and "raise to high rank"): if Brancha shouts for help, she will be like a man who "exalts" his enemy, who can then plan the destruction of the man who raised him. As the rest of the speech shows, this is a threat of violence against her.

453   our love] Royal plural, "my love".

460   blinde mate] "A blind Mate is, when one giveth check mate but seeth it not, yet it is neverthelesse a Mate, though a disgracefull one", *The Royall Game of Chesse-Play* (London 1656), p. 13. Here Middleton is rather twisting the chess-

terminology, for the sake of the double meaning.

470 loves flesh-flie by the silver wing] The violently opposite evocations of airy beauty ("silver wing") and of maggots in carrion ("flesh-flie") suggest powerfully the corruption of love. One might have expected it to be the woman that was caught in the spider's web, rather than "love's flesh-flie"; but Middleton's phrase implicates the victim in corruption as well as the seducer.

488 shew'd himself in's kind] "behaved according to his nature".

498 that fair] "that beauty".

546 Y'are a damn'd Baud] This is an aside hissed at Livia; but the contemptuous phrase about the Mother ("an old Ass go with you") is presumably heard only by the audience.

558–9 Water . . . after] A rhyme: see Dobson, pp. 984–5.

III. I

48 my fortune matcht me] Brancha talks as though she herself had had no say in the match: a convenient disregard of her own share of the responsibility for it.

61 by that copy] A reference to copyhold tenure, in which a man held land by custom of the manor, and had a copy of the court-rolls on which his rights were recorded. Brancha is maintaining her customary right to wrangle for anything she wants.

84 S.D. Enter LEANTIO] Since the action is continuous in place and time, I follow the original edition in not marking a new scene here, even though the stage is cleared of characters. Indeed, the original

may be right in not marking an exit for the Mother: she could remain visible on the upper stage while Leantio soliloquised below.

97 a Ditch side] The associations of *ditch* were a great deal more unsavoury than they are today: we must imagine something foul, stinking, and sewer-like.

121, 123 I have been better . . . I have been worse] Leantio takes these as referring to Brancha's health, but for her (and the audience) they have another meaning: she was better before she was unfaithful to her husband; she was worse at the actual moment of committing adultery.

129 *Florence*] For Brancha (and the audience) this also means "the Duke of Florence"; it was customary to call monarchs by the name of the territory that they ruled.

133 a tumbling cast] A throw in wrestling.

134 stands nothing to my minde] "Is not at all situated as I wish".

174 French cursie] "French curtsey": probably a reference to the effects of syphilis, the "French disease".

228 Knows me] Brancha momentarily interprets *know* as "have sexual intercourse with".

248 then] Probably = "then", not "than".

261 to my apprehension] "As it seemed to me". In fact it was Brancha who thought this, not the Mother (see I. III. 122–9).

306 a Colt in March-pain] Sweetmeats were commonly made into fancy shapes: cf. III. II. 82–3.

311–13 it begins . . . colour] "it begins to show colour (*i.e.* ripen) a little as soon as the sun . . . ."

331 Live in the issue] The argument takes an odd turn here; up to this

point, the ground of Leantio's envy has been that the man who keeps a mistress is not deeply engaged with her emotionally; but now he says that the drawback of marriage is that the children continue to be a nuisance after your wife has died.

III. II

2   I have invited her] Another sign that Guardiano lives at Livia's house, where the banquet is held (see III. I. 202–3).

45   *Rouans*] If the scribe copied Middleton's word without understanding it, the *u* perhaps represents a *v*; the place intended may be Rovezzano, just outside Florence to the east. There is no mention of the captainship in Malespini—another sign that he was not Middleton's immediate source, or at least not his sole one (see Critical Introduction p. 2).

82–3 Bull . . . Ram . . . Goat] *i.e.* sweetmeats in these shapes: *cf.* III. I. 306. The Ward unwittingly chooses horned creatures, the emblems of the cuckold.

129 brought up too] *i.e.* brought up to.

130 Cat and Trap] Cat, or tip-cat, was a game played with a small tapered piece of wood (the *cat*) and a stick (the *cat-stick*). The cat was *tipped*, *i.e.* struck at one end with the cat-stick and made to spring from the ground, and then driven away with a side-stroke. Trap, or trap-ball, was a similar game, but in this a ball was used, which was placed on the end of a wooden pivot (the *trap*). The player made the ball leap into the air by striking the other end of the trap with his *trap-stick*, and then drove it away.

144–7 pricksong . . . swell] For the

audience, the words carry sexual meanings of which the speaker is innocent.

170 *But . . . fresh*] The rhyme demands that the line should end at *blood*; but the correct lineation is by no means self-evident, so I have let the original reading stand.

172 *compound*] "come to an agreement" (*i.e.* to take her place).

204 who's] Perhaps a weak form of *whoso*; but it may be an error for *who*.

214 I stick closer to my self] "I persist more firmly in my resolve", or perhaps "I keep my self more to myself".

233 prick and praise] "success and its acknowledgment".

247 the Sinquapace, the Gay] *i.e.* "gay men dance the cinquepace". In the lines that follow, each dancer has some punning appropriateness.

278 In the speeches that follow, Leantio is not of course addressing Livia; it is not until line 309 that he comes to himself sufficiently to notice her.

396 It suits . . . breeding] Leantio has the courage to hold a military position, but does not belong to the right social class.

406 no greater loss] *i.e.* than loss of blood.

III. III

15   One your body, th'other your purse pays] Either the Ward would marry Isabella, or he would have to pay his guardian a large fine for refusing the wife tendered to him.

17   bolt] "arrow". There is an echo of the common proverb, "A fool's bolt is soon shot".

23   cri'd] "proclaimed as lost by the public crier" (Dyce).

24 Eggs o'th' spit] "Business in hand" (proverbial).

66 hearing] Probably a pun on *hear* and *hair*, which in some styles of speech were homophones: see Dobson, pp. 626, 643, 649.

70 of a very good last] "to a very good pattern". The reference is to a shoemaker's last.

75–6 A Nose . . . th'Camp] The reference is to the loss of the nose through venereal disease. Army camps were notorious for the number of prostitutes that hung around them.

86 catcht two in my lap] This has a sexual meaning, unperceived by the Ward. Isabella is coarsening.

125 rushes] These were strewn on floors (and on stages).

131 breed 'em all in your teeth] Dilke suggests that this refers to the belief that an affectionate husband had toothache while his wife was breeding.

IV. I

1 Watches] In the dialogue that follows, the clocks stand for various men, and setting your watch by a clock means sleeping with a man.

11 the Sun] *i.e.* the Duke. The sun was a standard image for the monarch.

19 here] "by my watch".

35 in sadness] "seriously".

54 legs] "bows, obeisances". In her reply, Brancha puns on the other meaning.

99 the great one] *i.e.* the Duke. The lines that follow are a veiled threat to murder Brancha and the Duke.

108 When the Moon hung so] Here Brancha probably makes horns at Leantio, mocking him as a cuckold. *Horned* was used of the crescent moon: *cf. Midsummer Night's Dream*, v.I. 233–6.

122 no greater] *Viz.* plague.

164 base] *i.e.* morally: referring to her pandering.

166 wrongs] "insults, imputations". The Duke is saying that people who behave scandalously (or whose relatives do) are the ones who are most sensitive about their reputations.

182 wastes] *i.e.* "she wastes".

184 house-keepers] People who keep open house: see note to II. I. 14–18.

193 He's a Factor] Not simply a statement of fact, but an expression of incredulous indignation at the idea of a member of his own family putting herself in the hands of a man of such inferior rank.

281 this Wall] *i.e.* his body.

287 not of their own] Because they use cosmetics.

298 grace] It is only through the grace of God that a man is able to repent his sins.

301–2 sorry . . . glory] The rhyme probably depends on a variant of *glory* with short *o*: see Dobson p. 484.

IV. II

4–10 Put case . . . Leacher] All Hippolito cares about is appearances: *honour* is not "virtue" but "reputation".

21 that glistring Whore] *i.e.* Brancha. His hurt pride still drives him to go to her to prove that he doesn't need her.

28 we are upon equal terms] Leantio had dealt him a blow by sleeping with his sister; Hippolito has requited him with a physical blow, thus making them all square.

57 Shift for thy self] "Make your escape".

61 thy sins] Hippolito's sins: Livia has turned from the body to the killer.

63 without voice] "silent, insidious".

90 All the world will grin] Like Hippolito, Guardiano is most concerned about appearances, the figure he will cut in the world.

107 Plumb-tree] "Plum tree", slang for the female pudenda.

109 open] A slang name for the medlar was "open-arse".

110 Medler-tree] The medlar is a small stone-fruit, eaten when rotten. It was also slang for a whore and for the female pudenda: cf. Romeo and Juliet, II. I. 33–6.

127 the going] The mill-mechanism, the "works".

132 singing in my head] A symptom of cuckoldry: cf. A Chaste Maid in Cheapside, I. II. 58.

140–1 I'ld fain . . . woman] She wishes that she could call Livia just "woman" instead of "aunt", i.e. that she were not related to her.

143 yon man] Hippolito.

176 all's] Dilke amends to all, but Dyce may be right in saying that it means "all as".

182–4 What . . . you] "What I am now, having returned to sense and judgment, is not the same person that rage and distraction . . . ."

203–4 time to come Will approve] Because she will learn of the splendid marriage that Hippolito's action has made possible for her. Approve means "demonstrate, show".

233 make one] "take part".

259–60 lies . . . suffice] A rhyme. In the holograph manuscript of A Game at Chess, Middleton regularly uses the spelling suffize, which presumably represents his own pronunciation. Cf. Dobson, pp. 927–30.

IV. III

43 when you leave this body] The argument takes an odd turn: at first the sanctuary was marriage, but has now become man's body.

V. I

4 I cannot wash . . . on't] Presumably because he feels his cuckold's horns.

15 your stamp shall go currant] Punning on stamp = "imprint on coin".

18 make you ready] "get dressed".

25 upon those] i.e. the spikes of the Galtrop.

32 If this . . .] Stand-by plots of this kind are not plausible, but are necessary if enough characters are to be killed off. Cf. the king's double plot (poisoned foil, poisoned drink) at the end of Hamlet.

V. II

43, 45 Sacrifice . . . dies] A rhyme: see note on IV. II. 259–60. In A Game at Chess, Middleton uses the spelling sacrifize.

55 S.D. Enter . . .] This masque has been arranged by Brancha for the purpose of poisoning the Cardinal. Hymen, god of marriage, was a common figure in wedding-masques, and was usually dressed in saffron. Ganymede, a beautiful youth, was cup-bearer to Zeus; his robe shows that Zeus made him into a constellation (Aquarius). Hebe, a goddess, was cup-bearer to the gods until displaced by Ganymede; her garment seems to represent the Milky Way.

66 Via Lactea] The Milky Way. Ganymede implies that Hebe had formed this by spilling a cup of

nectar; this is not the usual account in classical mythology, but Mulryne has shown that such a story was known in the 16th century.

69–70 sake . . . part] We should expect a rhyme; perhaps some lines have dropped out.

75   Antemask] An antimasque was a grotesque interlude between the acts of a masque; but here (as the spelling *Ante* shows) is given the meaning "something performed before a masque".

102 S.D. L I V I A *descends*] The Duke and the spectators are on the upper stage, while the masque is played below; Livia is presumably lowered from the "Heavens", but does not come right down to the main stage, for she later asks to be let down. She makes her long speech from somewhere above the altar, from which rise Isabella's poisoned fumes to kill her.

123 makes love take that] Prosperity is so powerful that he makes Love choose wealth. However, Dyce may be right in putting a mark of punctuation after *love*, so that *take that* becomes the utterance with which Juno throws down the "sign

of wealth".

125 S.D. "*treasure*"] Livia kills Isabella by throwing down to her the "sign of wealth", but it is not clear what this is. Mulryne calls attention to a manuscript annotation in the Yale University copy, in a 17th century hand, which says that Livia throws "flameing gold" on Isabella.

130 her lapful] Perhaps referring to Isabella's pregnancy (see IV. II. 80); or it may just be a reference to the "sign of wealth" that Livia has thrown down to her.

133 as cunningly] *i.e.* as cunningly as Isabella has been.

134 S.D. G U A R D I A N O *falls*] It is not clear how it happens that Guardiano is caught in his own trap. Perhaps Hippolito makes some unexpected noise, which the Ward mistakes for the signal, Guardiano having meantime inadvertently moved on to the trap-door as he prepares to entice Hippolito over.

152 How?] Not a request for information, but an exclamation— "What!".

223–4 foul . . . soul] A rhyme: see Dobson 691–2, 694.

BIBLIOGRAPHY

ABBREVIATIONS

M.L.N. = *Modern Language Notes*
M.L.Q. = *Modern Language Quarterly*
M.L.R. = *Modern Language Review*
P.Q. = *Philological Quarterly*
R.E.S. = *Review of English Studies*

I. WORKS BY MIDDLETON

COLLECTED AND SELECTED EDITIONS

Two New Playes. Viz. More Dissemblers besides Women. Women beware Women. Written by Tho. Middleton, Gent. London 1657.

Old Plays; Being a Continuation of Dodsley's Collection [ed. C. W. Dilke], vol. 5. London 1816.

The Works of Thomas Middleton, 5 vols, ed. Alexander Dyce. London 1840.

The Works of Thomas Middleton, 8 vols, ed. A. H. Bullen. London 1885–86.

Thomas Middleton, 2 vols, ed. Havelock Ellis: Mermaid Series, (contains ten plays). London 1887–90.

Elizabeth R. Jacobs, *A Critical Edition of Thomas Middleton's* WOMEN BEWARE WOMEN. Unpublished Thesis (University of Wisconsin) 1941.

J. R. Mulryne, *A Critical Edition of Thomas Middleton's "Women Beware Women"*. 2 vols. Unpublished Thesis (University of Cambridge) 1962.

Thomas Middleton, *Women Beware Women*, ed. Roma Gill. London (Benn) 1968.

II. CRITICAL STUDIES ETC.

A. GENERAL

1. *Critical*

BALD, R. C. "The Chronology of Middleton's Plays", in *M.L.R.*, XXXII (1937), pp. 33–43.

BARKER, R. H. *Thomas Middleton*. New York and London (Columbia U.P.; Oxford U.P.) 1958.

BRADBROOK, M. C. *Themes and Conventions of Elizabethan Tragedy*. (Cambridge U.P.) 1935

CHRIST, K. *Quellenstudien zu den Dramen Thomas Middletons*. Borna-Leipzig 1905.

ELLIS-FERMOR, U. M. *The Jacobean Drama*. Rev. ed. London (Methuen) 1958.

ELIOT, T. S. "Thomas Middleton", in *Selected Essays*. London (Faber) 1932.

HIBBARD, G. R. "The Tragedies of Thomas Middleton and the Decadence of the Drama", in *Nottingham Renaissance and Modern Studies* vol. I, pp. 35–64. Nottingham 1957.

JUMP, J. D. "Middleton's Tragedies", in *A Guide to English Literature: 2 The Age of Shakespeare*, ed. B. Ford, pp. 355-68. London (Penguin) 1955.

KNIGHTS, L. C. *Drama and Society in the Age of Johnson*. London (Chatto & Windus) 1937.

ORNSTEIN, R. *The Moral Vision of Jacobean Tragedy*. Wisconsin (Wisconsin U.P.) 1960.

PARKER, R. B. "Middleton's Experiments with Comedy and Judgment", in *Jacobean Theatre*, ed. J. R. Brown and B. Harris (*Stratford-upon-Avon Studies* I), pp. 178–99. London (Edward Arnold) 1960.

RIBNER, I. *Jacobean Tragedy*. London (Methuen) 1962.

SCHOENBAUM, S. *Middleton's Tragedies*. New York (Columbia U.P.) 1955.

STOLL, E. E. "Heroes and Villains: Shakespeare, Middleton, Byron, Dickens", in *R.E.S.*, XVIII (1942), pp. 257–69.

SYMONS, A. "Middleton and Rowley", in *The Cambridge History of English Literature*, ed. A. W. Ward and A. R. Waller, vol. VI. Cambridge (Cambridge U.P.) 1910.

TOMLINSON, T. B. *A Study of Elizabethan and Jacobean Tragedy*. Melbourne and London (Melbourne U.P.; Cambridge U.P.) 1964.

B. WOMEN BEWARE WOMEN

1. *Textual*

SIMPSON, P. "Thomas Middleton's 'Women beware Women.' ", in *M.L.R.*, XXXIII (1938), pp. 45–6.

2. *Critical*

COPE, J. I. "The Date of Middleton's *Women Beware Women*", in *M.L.N.*, LXXVI (1961), pp. 295–300.

DODSON, D. "Middleton's Livia", in *P.Q.*, XXVII (1948), pp. 376–81.

ENGELBERG, E. "Tragic Blindness in *The Changeling* and *Women Beware Women*", in *M.L.Q.*, XXIII (1962), pp. 20–28.

MAXWELL, B. "The Date of Middleton's *Women Beware Women*", in *P.Q.*, XXII (1943), pp. 338–42.

RIBNER, I. "Middleton's *Women Beware Women*: Poetic Imagery and the Moral Vision", in *Tulane Studies in English*, IX (1959), pp. 19–33.

RICKS, C. "Word-Play in *Women Beware Women*", in *R.E.S.*, (N.S.) XII (1961), pp. 238–50.

GLOSSARY

accompt	*account*, II. II. 180.
admiration	*wonder*, II. II. 10.
affect	*love*, II. I. 77 etc.
after	*at the rate of*, II. II. 87.
and	*if*, I. III. 13 etc.
angel	*gold coin worth ten shillings*, IV. II. 136.
anon	*soon*, II. II. 349, III. II. 41; (="coming, at your service") IV. II. 23.
apparent	*open*, IV. II. 9.
approve	*prove, demonstrate*, IV. II. 204, 230.
argument	*summary (of subject-matter of book, play, etc.)*, V. II. 37 etc.
artificially	*skilfully, deceivingly*, III. I. 277.
bag	*money-bag, purse*, I. I. 106.
banket	*banquet*, I. III. 33.
banquet	*a repast of sweetmeats, fruit, and wine*, III. I. 202 etc.
barren	*dull, unresponsive*, III. II. 64.
basilisk	*fabulous reptile which killed by its look*, IV. II. 149.
bate	*excuse, allow to be deficient in*, III. III. 78.
baud	*pander, procuress*, II. II. 546 etc.
benefit	*exemption (from jurisdiction of a court)*, III. II. 92.
bestead	*circumstanced*, III. II. 136.
bill (of parcels)	*invoice*, IV. I. 258.
blood	*blood-relationship, kindred*, II. I. 9; *passion, sexual desire*, IV. I. 190; *high birth*, I. III. 107.
brave	*richly dressed*, IV. I. 58; *fine, splendid*, IV. I. 70, 194.
brest	*singing-voice*, III. II. 142 etc.
brittle	*weak, fickle*, II. I. 189.
brood	*hatch*, II. II. 500.
buff	*ox-hide leather*, III. III. 75.
bum-roll	*stuffed cushion worn by women round the hips*, II. II. 147.
canaries	(a) *lively Spanish dance;* (b) *light sweet wines from the Canary Islands*, III. II. 250.
caroch	*stately kind of coach*, III. II. 270.
casting-bottle	*bottle for sprinkling perfumed waters*, III. I. 21, 38.
cat	*see note to* III. II. 130.
cater	*officer who bought the provisions in a large household*, III. III. 37.
cat-stick	*see note to* III. II. 130.
cleanly	*neat, clever*, III. III. 109.
close	*secret, hidden*, I. I. 96 etc.

closeness	*secrecy*, IV. II. 7.
cloth	cloth of silver: *tissue made of threads of silver interwoven with silk or wool*, IV. I. 65; cloth-stopple: *stopper made of cloth*, III. III. 99.
Coads-me	*an ejaculation expressing surprise*, I. II. 120.
coarse	*corpse*, III. II. 364.
come off	*extricate oneself*, II. II. 306.
comfit-maker	*confectioner*, III. III. 59.
commotion	*rebellion*, I. I. 82.
compass	*due limits*, I. I. 28.
conceit	*fancy, opinion*, I. III. 123; *meaning, signification*, V. II. 127.
conceive	*understand*, IV. II. 178, V. I. 26.
condition	*social rank*, I. I. 75; *personal quality*, II. II. 287.
confound	*destroy*, V. II. 151, 161.
conscionable	*scrupulous, showing regard for conscience*, IV. II. 6.
conveyance	*secret passage*, III. I. 277.
copy	*specimen of penmanship to be copied by a pupil*, IV. I. 145; *copyhold tenure*, III. I. 61 (see note).
course	*onset, encounter*, I. I. 90; *pack of dogs (in bear-baiting)*, IV. I. 101; *coarse*, III. III. 120; after the course of: *in accordance with the practice of*, I. I. 171.
curious	*finicky*, III. III. 38.
cursie	*curtsey*, III. I. 174, III. II. 228 S.D.
cutted	*rude, snappish*, III. I. 3.
cut-work	*kind of open-work embroidery or lace*, III. I. 20.
dab down	*duck down (?)*, III. III. 110.
dear	*grievous, earnest*, III. II. 293.
deft	*neat, trim*, III. II. 13.
design	*designate, indicate*, V. II. 100.
discover	*reveal*, V. II. 44, 73.
dislike	*displease*, III. I. 127.
down	*depressed, unhappy*, I. II. 208.
drab	*slattern*, II. II. 129.
draw	*entail, bring as a consequence*, IV. I. 255; *write out*, IV. II. 252.
drawn work	*fabric ornamented with patterns formed by drawing out some of the threads of warp or woof*, III. I. 19.
dry	(a) *thirsty*; (b) *sterile, frigid*, III. II. 94.
duke	*rook (in chess)*, II. II. 348 etc.
easily	*comfortably*, I. III. 113.
entail'd	*inalienably, permanently*, II. I. 96.
equal	*impartial*, III. II. 107.
ere	*ever*, I. I. 142 etc.; *before*, II. II. 340 etc.
even	*equally balanced*, V. II. 97.

factor   *agent employment by a merchant,* DR. PER., IV. I. 193.
factorship   *office or position as a "factor",* I. I. 165, III. II. 392.
fear   *frighten,* II. II. 418.
fetch over   *get the better of,* II. II. 456.
fit   *punish suitably,* III. I. 181.
flower   *flour,* III. I. 40.
fondness   *foolishness,* III. I. 170.
fool   *kind of custard, made with cream, eggs, and spices,* I. II. 136,
                        III. II. 138
forehead   *impudence, brazenness,* IV. I. 110.

gallant   *beautiful and fashionable woman,* II. II. 7.
galtrop   *caltrop, set of sharp spikes used against cavalry,* V. I. 5.
game   *sexual dalliance,* I. III. 9 etc.
gamester   *one addicted to amorous sport,* III. III. 103.
gardianer, gardiner: *guardian,* I. II. 113 etc.
get   *make money,* I. II. 116.
glorious   *proud, ostentatious,* III. I. 98.
go   *walk,* III. III. 105.
graffing   *grafting,* IV. II. 107.
guardiner   *guardian,* II. II. 107, 118.

halt   *be lame, be defective,* II. I. 96.
hand   *turn, "go",* I. II. 101.
hansell   *give earnest, advance payment, to,* I. II. 11.
hay   *kind of country-dance,* III. II. 248.
heat   *active phase, climax,* II. II. 265.
herse   *framework to carry tapers etc., placed over coffin in church, at
                        funerals,* III. II. 366.
hind'rance   *injury, incapacitation,* IV. II. 198.
hoboy   *oboe,* IV. III. S.D., 72.
hold   *bet, wager,* II. II. 353.
home   *thoroughly,* IV. I. 92; pay home: *punish, visit with retribution,*
                        IV. II. 86.
honor   *bow, curtsey,* III. II. 228 S.D.
hopper rumpt   *with a behind like a seed-basket,* II. II. 127.
humane   *human,* I. II. 206.

I   *aye, yes,* I. II. 106 etc.
ignorantly   *unwittingly, inadvertently,* V. II. 193.
innocent   *simpleton, half-wit,* III. III. 22.
invention   *literary composition,* IV. II. 223.

jiggam-bob   *knick-knack,* II. II. 83.

key   *quay,* I. III. 17.
kickshaws   *fancy dish (in cookery),* I. II. 47.

leave   *stop, desist from*, II. II. 181.
lie in   *remain in prison*, I. II. 197.
lift   *attack, blow*, II. I. 39.
light   *arrive*, II. I. 68, III. I. 72; *fall, land*, IV. II. 85.
like   *please*, II. I. 143, III. I. 13.
list   *choose, please*, II. II. 104 etc.; *listen*, II. II. 39 etc.

mad   *extraordinary* (?), *hilarious* (?), III. III. 113.
mar'l   *marvel*, I. II. 133.
match   *see* set match.
mean   *of low rank*, IV. I. 257.
measures   *a grave or stately dance*, III. II. 247.
meat   *food*, III. III. 24.
meer   *complete, utter*, II. I. 161 etc.
meerly   *completely, utterly*, I. II. 156.
mends   *amends, reparation*, II. II. 279; *legal remedy*, III. II. 96.
model   *synopsis of a literary work*, V. II. 34.
motion'd (of)   *proposed, suggested* (*by*), II. II. 293.

necessities   *poverty*, II. II. 444.
neerness   *relatedness*, I. I. 120.

oddes   *difference*, II. I. 163.
once   *for once*, III. II. 253.
otherways   *otherwise*, IV. II. 191 etc.
out   *at fault, at a loss*, II. II. 266.

parcel   *item* (*of an invoice*), IV. I. 257.
pay   *punish, bring retribution on*, V. II. 49.
pillowber   *pillow-case*, IV. II. 135.
pitch out   *pay out* (?), I. II. 132.
plot   *synopsis of a literary work*, V. II. 136; the plot's full: *the play is fully cast*, IV. II. 234.
poyse   *weight*, IV. I. 165.
present   *immediate*, V. II. 194; *readily available*, V. I. 30.
presently   *immediately*, II. II. 371, IV. II. 25.
prethee   *prithee, I pray you*, I. II. 120 etc.
pricksong   *singing at sight*, III. II. 144.
prodigious   *portentous, monstrous*, V. II. 184.
professor   *somebody that follows some art or science as a profession*, III. III. 39; *member of a religious order*, IV. III. 58.
purchase   (a) *acquisition*, (b) *booty*, I. I. 13.
put up   *submit to*, I. I. 159.

quean   *whore*, II. II. 186; *hussy*, IV. II. 112.
querister   *chorister*, IV. II. 131.
quicken   *be conceived, receive life*, III. I. 263.

| quit | *requite,* V. II. 139. |
| quoth'a | *he said,* IV. II. 106. |

rate	after the rate of: *in accordance with,* I. I. 97, 137; *in the style of,* III. I. 43.
reach	*understand,* V. II. 170.
remove	*depart, die,* V. II. 241.
resolv'd	(a) *satisfied,* (b) *resolute,* IV. II. 190.
respective for	*attentive to, careful about,* I. III. 49.
rest	*remain,* IV. II. 150.
right	*rite,* III. II. 114; *straight,* III. III. 102.
ropes	*the tight-rope,* III. III. 124.
round	*kind of dance, in which performers move in a ring,* III. II. 249.
roundly	*thoroughly, briskly,* I. I. 114.

sack-posset	*drink made from hot milk curdled with sack (white wine from Spain and the Canaries),* I. II. 136.
sallet	*salad-herb, lettuce,* III. II. 59.
sand-box	*box with perforated top for sprinkling sand (as a blotter),* IV. II. 137.
scaffold	*raised platform or stand for holding spectators,* III. III. 114.
second	*aid,* II. II. 333
sent	*scent,* III. I. 89.
set match	like a set match: *as if by agreement or conspiracy,* V. II. 168.
she	*woman,* II. I. 40.
shittlecock	*the game of (battledore and) shuttlecock,* III. III. 83.
show like	*look like,* I. III. 74.
simple	*slight,* III. III. 130; simple charge: *sheer expense,* I. I. 89.
simply	*absolutely,* IV. I. 48.
sinquapace	*cinquepace, kind of lively dance,* III. II. 247, IV. II. 133.
smack	*taste,* I. III. 6; *kiss,* II. II. 125.
spake	*spoken,* I. I. 130.
spare	*be niggardly,* II. I. 16; *withhold, hoard,* III. II. 321.
sparkle	*spark,* IV. I. 251.
sped	*in bad plight,* V. II. 139; sped of: *provided with,* IV. I. 170, 172.
speeding	*dispatching, deadly,* V. II. 158.
spoil	*destroy, kill,* V. II. 149.
sprig	*ornament in the form of a sprig,* III. II. 15.
spring	*springe,* V. II. 171.
start	*startle,* II. I. 148, 157.
start up	*upstart,* IV. I. 127.
state	*estate, possessions,* III. I. 26; *stateliness, magnificence,* IV. II. 246; *ruling body, magnates,* I. III. 79 etc.; states: *nobility, dignitaries,* I. III. 110, 117 S.D.
stick	*hesitate, scruple,* I. I. 181.
still	*always,* I. I. 35 etc.

stool-ball	*country game resembling cricket, played mainly by young women,* III. III. 84.
stoop	*condescend,* I. II. 131.
stove	*hot-air bath, sweating-room,* IV. I. 318.
stranger	*non-relative, one not a kinsman,* II. I. 14; *foreigner,* II. II. 252 etc.; *visitor, guest,* II. II. 195; (adj.) *unrelated, not kin,* I. II. 81.
strike by	*consign to oblivion* (?), III. II. 261.
success	*fortune (good or bad),* I. I. 141.
sucket	*succade, candied fruit,* III. I. 306
swindg	*freedom, impetus,* I. I. 98.
take	*bring,* II. II. 483; take care: *be concerned, wonder,* III. I. 111; take out: *copy,* I. I. 100.
taste	*feel, experience,* V. II. 160; *detect,* IV. III. 28.
tender'd	*cherished,* III. I. 51.
then	*than,* I. I. 6 etc.
through	*completely, fully,* IV. I. 62.
thrum	*waste time,* III. III. 16.
timber	fine timber'd: *well built,* III. II. 208.
tipping	*the knocking up of the cat at tip-cat,* I. II. 110. See note to III. II. 130.
to	*in addition to,* II. II. 411.
toll	*draw, entice,* V. II. 132.
too	*to,* I. I. 60, I. II. 84 etc.
touch	keep true touch: *act faithfully, behave as one should,* V. II. 106.
towards	*imminent,* II. I. 88.
trap, trap-stick	see note to III. II. 130.
trick	*trinket, knick-knack,* II. II. 83; trick up: *adorn, dress up,* II. II. 71 etc.
triumph	*pageant,* "*show*", V. I. 8, V. II. 183.
trow	*do you think?,* II. II. 54, III. II. 76.
turtle	*turtle-dove,* II. II. 378.
unkindly	*unnatural,* II. I. 10.
unvalued	*priceless,* I. I. 13, III. II. 183.
verjuyce	*the acid juice of sour fruit (e.g. crab-apples) used in cooking,* III. III. 50.
vilde	*vile,* III. II. 320.
wear	*were,* V. I. 3.
whether	*whither,* III. I. 293.
woodcock	*simpleton, fool,* III. III. 22.
worm-wood water	*bitter-tasting cordial prepared from wormwood* II. II. 558.